ARE YOU SURE IT'S

ARTHRITIS?

ARE YOU SURE IT'S ARTHRITIS?

A Guide to Soft-Tissue Rheumatism

PAUL DAVIDSON, M.D.

Macmillan Publishing Company

NEW YORK

Illustrations by Susan Quan

Macmillan Publishing Company
866 Third Avenue, New York, N.Y. 10022
Collier Macmillan Canada, Inc.

Library of Congress Cataloging in Publication Data
Davidson, Paul, 1931 Jan. 6–
Are you sure it's arthritis?
Includes index.
1. Nonarticular rheumatism. 2. Connective tissues—Diseases. 3. Muscles—Diseases. I. Title. [DNLM: 1. Connective Tissue Diseases. 2. Rheumatism. WE 544 D253a]
RC927.5.N65D38 1985 616.7'22 85-13668
ISBN 0-02-529770-8

Macmillan books are available at special discounts for bulk purchases for sales promotions, premiums, fund-raising, or educational use. For details, contact:

Special Sales Director
Macmillan Publishing Company
866 Third Avenue
New York, N.Y. 10022

10 9 8 7 6 5 4 3 2 1

Designed by Jack Meserole

Printed in the United States of America

This book is not intended as a substitute for the medical advice of physicians. The reader should regularly consult a physician in matters relating to his or her health and particularly in respect of any symptoms that may require diagnosis or medical attention.

Contents

Acknowledgments

The preparation of this book would have been very difficult without the assistance and support of many people. I thank my wife Ursula and children Daniel and Julie for their patience. My deepest appreciation for suggestions from Drs. Martin A. Shearn, Tracy A. Newkirk, and John A. Buehler, and for the reference material obtained by Katherine Renick and Julie Kahl. My thanks to Joseph Eszterhas and Dorothy Panella for their moral support.

My special thanks to Suzanne Lipsett for her editorial suggestions.

Last but not least, my gratitude to all of my patients from whom I learned so much.

Introduction

At one point or another in our lifetimes, we will all have aches and pains in our muscles or joints. These discomforts may be transient or permanent. They may be mild or severe, a nuisance or a disability. Such complaints are usually diagnosed as arthritis, a group of conditions that can cause permanent damage to the joints and pain that is difficult to treat.

Often, though, the problem is not arthritis but one of many conditions that resemble it. These disorders, known as *soft-tissue rheumatism,* affect not the joints but many of the soft connecting tissues of the body—the tendons, joint capsules, ligaments, fascias, bursas, cartilages, and muscles. Significantly, soft-tissue rheumatism in most of its manifestations responds much more readily to treatment and pain therapy than arthritis. Therefore, a delayed diagnosis based on the resemblance between the two kinds of illnesses can have great import for people with soft-tissue rheumatism. If the conditions of these patients go unrecognized for what they are, they might miss out on direct treatment that could effectively—and often quickly—eradicate their suffering.

Though soft-tissue rheumatism is less well known to the general public than arthritis, its frequency is truly staggering. For example, a recent Mayo Clinic review of the diagnoses of twenty-one thousand patients seen in their outpatient physical therapy department in 1977 turned up a dismaying number of cases of soft-tissue rheumatism. Many disorders were represented in this sample—injuries, strokes, blood vessel ailments, neurological problems, arthritis, rheumatism, and many other diseases. In fully one-third of the cases, however, the diagnosis was soft-tissue rheumatism. Reports published in the prestigious medical journal *Arthritis and Rheumatism* showed the same high incidence of soft-tissue rheumatism in patients seen in offices of rheumatologists in both the United States and Mexico.

The problem is by no means restricted to our own hemisphere, however. Soft-tissue rheumatism is found worldwide, in dry and wet climates, in flatlands and mountainous country, and ranks among the greatest causes of disability in our global work force.

This disease has no respect for age, sex, or race. It can occur in schoolchildren, athletes, mature adults, and the elderly. It has even been seen in newborn babies. Still, certain forms of soft-tissue rheumatism strike identifiable groups with particular frequency. Physically active people are prone to such forms of the disease as tendinitis, bursitis, and fasciitis. Sedentary workers and people under stress are more likely to develop fibrositis. Those over fifty years of age are targets for polymyalgia rheumatica and giant cell arteritis. The injured are candidates for reflex sympathetic dystrophy.

What significance do these facts hold for you? Why learn about these diseases? To answer these questions, perhaps more questions are in order. For example, did you pick up this book because you are trying to solve the mystery of your own lingering muscular discomfort? Might you, after reading this book, have reason to attribute your aches and pains—or those of someone you care about—to soft-tissue rheumatism? Have you been wondering if it is possible to prevent some of these disorders? Or if it is always necessary to see a doctor when you have muscular pain? Do you need to know what you can do yourself to help relieve your pain and discomfort?

The purpose of this book is to answer all such questions. The book is not meant to teach you complete self-diagnosis and treatment, since some of the soft-tissue rheumatic disorders can lead to severe pain and disability calling for medical expertise, and certain forms, if untreated by a knowledgeable physician, can even lead to blindness and death. Rather, the book is meant to guide your thinking: in determining whether you might have soft-tissue rheumatism, in practicing self-help to prevent and treat minor ailments, and in becoming alert to when you *must* see your doctor.

The conditions we call arthritis and rheumatism are of great concern to us all. As with any disease, our first line of defense against these illnesses is the knowledge that dispels our fear of the unknown. This book is intended to convey, clearly and simply, such basic information on soft-tissue rheumatism that has until now remained virtually unknown to the general public.

PAUL DAVIDSON, M.D.

November, 1985

ARE YOU SURE IT'S ARTHRITIS?

I

The Hidden Diseases: Soft-Tissue Rheumatism

TO EVERYONE WITH ACHES AND PAINS

If you have ever had aches or pains—and who hasn't?—there is a high probability that some of them were caused by one or more of the disorders discussed in this book. This group of ailments is responsible for at least one-third of all reported musculoskeletal pains. Further, the diseases in this group constitute a major cause of activity limitation and physical disability worldwide. For more than a century this cluster has been given many names, but none describes these conditions better than *soft-tissue rheumatism.*

Despite the high incidence of soft-tissue rheumatism, lay people and medical professionals alike tend to think first of arthritis when aches and pains are a chronic symptom. This is not because the soft-tissue rheumatic diseases are unknown or unstudied; rather, in many cases they go unrecognized for what they are. They frequently mimic arthritis and can be mistaken for it, especially since it is possible in the early stages of arthritis to have no X-ray or laboratory abnormalities, which is also true of most soft-tissue diseases. When the soft-tissue rheumatic disorders occur *with* arthritis, they are even more likely to be treated as arthritic pains—in the same way that people are often known by the company they keep. And where the soft-tissue disorders do generate abnormalities seen on X rays and laboratory tests, a physician not widely experienced with them could confuse them with arthritic symptoms and disorders. For all these reasons, then, I refer to soft-tissue rheumatism as "the hidden diseases."

ARTHRITIS VERSUS RHEUMATISM

Because the well-known and well-publicized arthritic diseases are often the screen that hides soft-tissue rheumatism, it is important to focus on the differences between the two sets of conditions. The most important reason—and the one having the most practical implications for everyone with aches and pains—is that soft-tissue rheumatism is often more easily and successfully treated than arthritis. In many cases, with proper treatment, the pain of the soft-tissue rheumatic diseases can be completely relieved, which is less likely in the case of arthritis. But proper treatment depends on accurate diagnosis, and this in turn depends on a deeper understanding of the soft-tissue disorders than has so far been prevalent. This book is specifically intended to increase that understanding.

Despite some superficial similarities, arthritis and soft-tissue rheumatism differ significantly in many ways with respect to cause, course, treatment, and outlook. If you or your loved ones have aches and pains, there are some good reasons for you to know these differences. And if you have been diagnosed as having arthritis, you could begin to suspect, by reading this book, that some of your symptoms might be due to soft-tissue rheumatism. The days of the passive patient are over. You can benefit in many practical ways by learning all you can about your condition. This is not to advocate self-diagnosis and self-treatment over medical supervision; it is, rather, to argue for self-education and the uninhibited sharing of information.

In general, knowing that soft-tissue rheumatism, in its many forms, exists at all will give you some insight into what are often mistakenly considered merely vague and indefinable discomforts and miseries by all except the sufferers themselves. Also, knowing that the outlook for soft-tissue rheumatism is better than that of arthritis can give you some peace of mind. Whereas the pain of arthritis is often stubborn, in many instances that of soft-tissue rheumatism can be completely eradicated. Clearly, learning about these "hidden" diseases and how they differ from arthritis can be of immense practical value in the everyday lives of people with aches and pains.

Both soft-tissue rheumatism and arthritis can cause aching, pain, stiffness, and disability. But that is where the similarity ends. Soft-tissue rheumatism affects the "soft tissues" of our bodies—the muscles, tendons, ligaments, and the like (see the following chapter and the glossary for definitions of these terms). Arthritis affects the "hard tissues"—our joints and their cartilages. These distinct diseases may occur separately, as suggested earlier, or they can be present simultaneously. The term *arthritis* is a precise one derived from the Greek word *arthron,* meaning "joint," and the suffix *-itis,* meaning "inflammation." The term *rheumatism,* on the other hand, is not as clear-cut. It stems from the Greek word *rheumatismos,* meaning "suffering from a flux." It is generally used rather loosely to refer to numerous conditions characterized by pain and inflammation in joints, muscles, and fibrous tissue. Therefore, the term *rheumatism* actually includes both arthritis and soft-tissue rheumatism, and as such isn't a very precise word. *Soft-tissue rheumatism,* though still a general term, refers to a category of diseases that cause aches and pains, that differ from the arthritic disorders, and that affect the soft tissues, not the joints. Confusingly, I might add that if you go to an arthritis clinic, you will be seen by a rheumatologist.

You have probably heard of many of the names given to various forms of arthritis, such as osteoarthritis (so-called degenerative arthritis), rheumatoid arthritis, gout, and ankylosing spondylitis. Again, these are diseases that affect and cause damage to joints.

Just as there are many forms of arthritis, so there are many forms of soft-tissue rheumatism. Some of the more well-known types are *tennis elbow* and *shoulder bursitis.* These are forms of *tendinitis*—inflammation of the tendons—and they result in localized pains. Many more conditions in the tendinitis group cause pains in other parts of the body; for example, *trochanteric bursitis* causes hip pain, *plantar fasciitis* causes heel pain, and *anserine bursitis* causes knee pain.

Other forms of soft-tissue rheumatism that cause more diffuse aching, pain, and stiffness are far less well known, despite their widespread occurrence in every country in the world. One of these, *fibrositis,* causes considerable pain and stiffness, although laboratory tests on its sufferers routinely come out normal. This disorder is one of the rheumatic conditions whose origins lie in the delicate balance between mind and body.

Polymyalgia rheumatica may mimic fibrositis but is a distinct disease. It can cause severe pain, stiffness, and disability, but with proper treatment even months of suffering can be reversed within twenty-four hours. *Giant cell arteritis* is yet another soft-tissue disease that can cause severe musculoskeletal aches and pains; in some cases it causes blindness as well. Again, this condition generally responds completely to the correct therapy. And *causalgia,* or *reflex sympathetic dystrophy,* is a disease that can occur following even a trivial injury, causing severe disability to a limb. At times causalgia can be prevented from developing; where it does occur it can be successfully treated—if accurately diagnosed.

All these forms of soft-tissue rheumatism will be discussed in detail in subsequent chapters. But to gain a deeper understanding of the effects of these diseases on individuals' lives, let's take a closer look at the specific symptoms associated with particular soft-tissue rheumatic conditions.

THE FACES OF SOFT-TISSUE RHEUMATISM

Soft-tissue rheumatism wears many faces. It may announce its presence by stiffness alone, a symptom ranging in intensity from barely noticeable to severely inhibiting. Stiffness can keep sufferers from rising from their chairs or putting on their own shoes and socks. The actual aches and pains stemming from this group of diseases run the gamut from minor nuisance to agonizing disability.

The overall effects of these diseases can be almost inconsequential to afflicted individuals, or they can result in high fevers, blindness, and even death. Such a disease may be insidious in onset or strike like a lightning bolt. And it may be easy to recognize or almost defy diagnosis.

I could list symptoms and try to describe their intensities almost endlessly where soft-tissue rheumatism is concerned, but more telling by far are real-life descriptions of actual sufferers. The following case histories are typical of the problems seen by rheumatologists and other physicians throughout the world. If your own aches and pains have led you to read this book, perhaps one of these scenarios will seem familiar to you.

You're thirty-two years old and a meticulous housekeeper with two young children who keep you busy all day. To stay fit you used to attend a dance-exercise class, but lately you haven't had time. Your relationship with your husband has become a little shaky, and the family finances have been increasingly troublesome. You and your husband finally decide that you should put the children in day-care and take a full-time job. You find a good secretarial position and enter your new life-style optimistically. All goes fairly well for a while, but you begin to have aches and pains in your upper back and shoulders, and pain and stiffness when you get up in the morning. To make matters worse, you develop headaches, a tingling in your arms, and feelings of swelling in your hands. You're frightened—perhaps it's arthritis or something even worse. You're not sure you'll be able to hide your distress at work for much longer, and you worry about becoming completely disabled by the pain. How will you ever keep your household running when you can hardly get yourself out of bed? Your physician examines you, orders X rays and blood studies, and finds nothing abnormal. He feels you are overtired and suggests that you get more rest and take aspirin for your symptoms. But your symptoms persist and grow worse, and soon you begin to wonder if they're all in your mind. At this point you're reluctant to go back to your doctor; instead, you begin trying various diets and vitamin regimes, all to no avail. You find it hard to believe that all this misery is in your mind, and you are absolutely correct. You have a common problem called fibrositis, and there are effective forms of treatment available.

Being handy around the house, you decide to refinish an old table. After sanding half the top, your fingers ache a bit, while your right elbow gets so sore that you have to stop working. In fact, the elbow pain gets so bad that you can hardly open a door, lift a cup, or even shake hands, and it doesn't go away. Weeks go by with no improvement. You don't play tennis, so it can't be tennis elbow. You must have arthritis, right? Wrong. It *is* tennis elbow, and with a simple treatment you're fine again.

You're forty-eight years old, active, and have never been a complainer, so the slight ache in your left hip doesn't concern you at first. The pain increases, however, and you find it ever more difficult to go up and down stairs, get up from your chair, and get into your car. Then the pain begins to make sleep difficult, since lying on your left side becomes impossible. You really get concerned when you learn that your forty-six-year-old friend has to get his hip replaced because of arthritis. You rush to your doctor and have your hip X-rayed. The result is perfectly normal—no arthritis at all. What you have is a nasty case of trochanteric bursitis, which can be relieved with appropriate treatment.

You have a good marriage, healthy children, and no financial problems. Ceramics is your passion, and you have time to pursue it. Life is beautiful until your hands begin to ache. At first you have to stop working every so often to give your hands a rest; in time you can do no ceramics at all, and the lost time frustrates you beyond belief. Soon your right hand gets much worse, and severe pains like electric shocks begin to shoot down into your fingers. During the night the pains are so severe that you can hardly sleep. Then you notice that you lack feeling in your index and middle fingers. Arthritis runs in your family. You hope yours will go away, but it doesn't. You become depressed as you begin to think you'll never work in your studio again. Finally you go to your doctor for the bad news. Surprisingly, it's good news you hear: Your problem is not uncommon, and it's not arthritis. You have the carpal tunnel syndrome, a condition due to pressure on a major nerve going to your hand. Depending on the severity, it can be cured by either an injection or a simple surgical procedure.

Perhaps you've picked up an inch or two around the waistline and decide that you had better get into shape. Jogging is the answer. All goes well and you're feeling great and losing a few pounds. But one day you go out jogging and find that the back of your ankle begins to hurt. The pain is so bad that you have to limp, and finally you give up jogging for a while. The pain decreases a bit so you begin to jog again, only to have the pain return with a vengeance. Arthritis? Not at all: You have Achilles' tendinitis.

You've had good health for sixty-four years, and you're proud of it. You don't smoke or drink; you eat properly and get a moderate amount of exercise. But your muscles suddenly begin to feel very stiff after you've been sleeping or sitting for a while. It's hard to get out of bed or out of a chair, and your wife has to help you on with your shoes and socks. Now you begin to feel a generalized aching along with increasing stiffness, and your scale shows that you've lost a few pounds. After a month of this, you really start worrying: Perhaps you have arthritis or maybe even cancer. You haven't seen a doctor in years, and you decide that now is the time. You have many studies done, all of which are normal except one. It's a blood test called a sedimentation rate: Your rate is 90, which is distinctly abnormal. The doctor diagnoses your condition not as arthritis or cancer but as polymyalgia rheumatica, a disease you've never heard of. You take the prescribed pills, and within twenty-four hours you feel a little better. Within four days you're feeling completely normal.

Perhaps you do smoke a bit too much, but so does your father. He's seventy-five years old and doesn't have heart disease or high blood pressure. You're forty-four and keep in shape by swimming a mile a day. One day while swimming you get a pain in your chest that goes away when you rest. It begins to occur with regularity when you swim short distances, and you naturally think you might have angina pectoris, or heart disease. You hate to give up swimming, but out of concern you begin babying yourself, hoping that the pain will go away. Still, worry overcomes you and you go to your doctor for a complete physical exam, an electrocardiogram, and an exercise tolerance test. You pass them all with flying colors. The doctor then shows you which motions bring on the pain and explains that you have, not heart disease, but a nuisance condition—that is, a minor irritation of no great significance to your health called *costochondritis,* known as one of the "chest wall syndromes." With this knowledge, you relax for the first time in months. You start swimming again, and the pain doesn't seem so bad.

You're a saleswoman in a large department store. Just after the spring rush at work, you notice a pain in your wrist, on the side where your thumb is. It gets worse, and you begin to use the other hand to open doors, choose clothes off the rack, and lift packages. Wrapping packages and writing up receipts become major ordeals. Resting the hand and wrist doesn't help. The pain begins to awaken you at night, and you lie in bed wondering how you're going to keep your job. You're afraid to see the doctor because you think you might be getting arthritis. But when you finally can avoid it no longer, you learn that you have a common form of rheumatism known as De Quervain's tenosynovitis, which is easily treated.

Taking inventory at the pharmacy was grueling, but you finally finished on time. Your right knee had begun to hurt about halfway through, and initially you thought it was due to too much kneeling. Now the pain is worse, and you're starting to limp. A chiropractor tells you that your spine is misaligned and performs a series of spinal manipulations, all to no avail. Then you see a rheumatologist; he finds that your knee X ray is normal and tells you that although arthritis or a torn knee cartilage are still possibilities, the examination suggests a less serious diagnosis: anserine bursitis, a slight inflammation immediately below the knee joint. The rheumatologist gives you an injection of an anesthetic and one of a cortisone derivative into the tender area. The pain disappears immediately.

At the age of seventy-two, you recall having had a few headaches in your life but nothing as persistent as this one. You try all the remedies advertised on television without gaining any relief at all. After a week, you notice that you have a fever and wonder whether you have the flu. You don't improve but soon begin to develop aching in your muscles and joints. Now you feel just terrible—it's surely some type of infection, you think. Not one to run to your doctor for every ache and pain, you decide to call her and avoid the office visit. She wisely refuses to diagnose your condition over the telephone and urges you to come in. Give it a few days, you tell yourself. The next morning you again awaken with a throbbing headache and to your horror cannot see out of your left eye. You rush to the doctor's office, and she immediately suspects a condition known as temporal, cranial, or giant cell arteritis. She immediately sends you to the hospital for a biopsy of an artery in your temporal area and begins treatment with prednisone. The diagnosis is confirmed. You learn that the disorder you have can appear with many different symptoms and that if you had seen your doctor earlier, the blindness in your eye, now irreversible, could have been prevented.

While doing carpentry in your house, you slip on the floor and twist your ankle. It hurts and swells a little bit, so you have to limp. You feel more comfortable not moving the ankle at all, and you try to protect it. After three days, the pain starts to increase. A few more days go by, and the ankle and foot are red, swollen, perspiring, and unbearably painful. Even the pressure of the bedsheets is intolerable. You see your physician, and he initially suspects an infectious arthritis. He puts you in the hospital and treats you with an antibiotic, but the studies he ordered do not confirm a diagnosis of infectious arthritis. Despite the treatment, your misery continues with no relief. Even narcotics only dull the pain. Your doctor calls in a consultant who diagnoses your condition as reflex sympathetic dystrophy, or causalgia. She explains that this unusual condition can follow even the most minor of injuries, and if untreated can lead to a thinning of the bones in the affected areas along with severe degeneration of the muscles. With the proper medications and intensive physical therapy, however, you make a full recovery.

THE INCIDENCE OF RHEUMATISM

The sketches above suggest the variety of forms that soft-tissue rheumatic diseases can take. Viewed individually, these conditions cause everything from persistent irritation to painful life-disrupting handicaps. Seen from a worldwide perspective, the amount of human suffering and disability caused by soft-tissue rheumatism is truly staggering. There are an estimated 12 million sufferers in the United States alone.

Though this figure is a reliable estimate, for many reasons it is difficult to ascertain the exact incidence of these diseases. For one thing, many sufferers of minor aches and pains never see a doctor. Also, in many surveys soft-tissue disorders are often lumped with arthritis and called by its name. In many other instances they are mistakenly diagnosed as arthritis. Finally, neither soft-tissue rheumatism nor arthritis are among the diseases that medical practitioners must report to local and state health departments, as are, for example, tuberculosis, syphilis, and typhoid fever. We have far more accurate statistics on the incidence of cancer because of very close monitoring by hospital, university, and national centers. Still, enough information is available to support my claim that 36 million Americans suffer from arthritis and rheumatism and that approximately one-third of those, or 12 million people, have soft-tissue rheumatism.[1] But who are the people whose lives are interrupted by these often disabling diseases? We will now turn to this question.

THE AFFLICTED

It's not possible to construct a portrait of a particular kind of person who might be susceptible to soft-tissue rheumatism, but we can say something about vulnerable individuals on the basis of such factors as age, sex, occupation, diet, geographical location, and race.

Let's consider age first. Tendinitis-type afflictions and fibrositis can occur anytime from the preteen years through old age. But in all age categories these disorders are most likely to occur in people who are very active, intense, and productive. There is no question that the incidence of soft-tissue rheumatism grows with increasing age. Polymyalgia rheumatica and giant cell arteritis, for example, are rarely found in people younger than fifty years of age. But no age group is completely free of these conditions.

The type of occupation or activities a person is involved in has a strong bearing on the kind of soft-tissue rheumatic problems he might develop. For instance, if you use your hands in frequent repetitive motions, the tendons of your fingers or wrists stand a good chance of becoming inflamed. Such conditions are often seen in, for example, piano or stringed instrument players, hairdressers, mechanics, butchers, and typists. Elbow and shoulder problems are common among laborers, ball players, tennis players, and golfers. Desk workers and others engaged in tension-related occupations are particularly subject to fibrositis and neck-muscle tension pains that result in headaches. Athletes are subject to Achilles' tendinitis and other rheumatic disorders affecting both the upper and lower extremities. Many other parts of the body become involved when they are particularly stressed. However, I do not mean to imply that only specific activities cause certain problems, for it often happens that no relationship is apparent between the physical problem and the afflicted person's occupation. Furthermore, these disorders often involve first one area, then another. And many people are particularly susceptible to the simultaneous involvement of multiple sites. In fact, just such a situation of multiple sites often leads both patient and physician to believe initially that a generalized arthritic condition such as rheumatoid arthritis, and not a soft-tissue rheumatic condition, is present.

The question of whether diet is a factor in soft-tissue rheumatism has yet to be resolved. A review of the arguments on both sides would require a separate book, but I will offer my own opinion here. Having spoken with and treated patients from all parts of the world, I've never been convinced that one or another diet makes a significant difference in the causation of rheumatism. The same soft-tissue rheumatic problems occur with high frequency among the well-fed and the malnourished, the meat eaters and the vegetarians, the "junk food addicts" and the organic health food consumers. In fact, I have been surprised at how *few* such symptoms result from poor nutrition and out-and-out malnutrition. Diet may well play a role in the treatment of soft-tissue rheumatism, but as yet this has not been adequately demonstrated.

What about geographic location and race? Many people in this country seem to believe that groups in other parts of the world are relatively immune to these aches and pains. They attribute the differences to a relative lack of stress and to dietary, religious, or climatic factors. There are regional differences in the distribution patterns of these illnesses, but I have yet to see or hear about a group that is immune to soft-tissue rheumatism. My travels have taken me to some of the most primitive places in the world and to some of the most sophisticated—in Europe, Asia, the Middle East, and Central America—and there I have found that same high incidence of soft-tissue rheumatic problems. Japan and Western Europe, for example, are filled with spas for the treatment of these disorders. Further, in Europe and the Middle East, there are many ruins of spas that date back to Roman times, strongly suggesting that the rheumatic problems we experience and treat were not unknown to older cultures, since hot baths often give temporary relief of musculoskeletal pains.

I recently returned from doing some volunteer work in a

small isolated village in western Guatemala. Most of the people in this area are indigenous, being descendants of the Mayas, and now work on the many coffee plantations. After the *padre* in the village had spread the word that there was a specialist in arthritis and rheumatism at the clinic, the number of clinic visits rose dramatically. Large numbers of men and women appeared with soft-tissue rheumatic complaints identical to those I see in my practice in Marin County, California.

Finally, at the various rheumatology meetings I have attended, I have met and spoken with arthritis specialists from all over the world, including those from the Iron Curtain countries. Their experiences have been little different from my own. So, it appears that soft-tissue rheumatism dates back to antiquity, affects people of diverse cultures, and occurs worldwide. If we project our estimate of 12 million American sufferers onto a global scale, the extent of the physical distress involved—the discomfort, pain, and loss of work potential—becomes truly formidable. For this reason, the need to spread what is known of these usually treatable though little-known conditions becomes vitally important.

2

Where, Why, and What?

WHERE? A BIT OF ANATOMY

It will be helpful to know some simple anatomy as we explore the different forms of rheumatism. I will describe the difference between "hard tissues" and "soft tissues"—namely, the bones and joints versus the muscles, tendons, joint capsules, ligaments, bursas, and fascias. Let's take a look at the hard tissues first.

The Bones and Joints

The bones form the framework of the body. In an adult, there are 206 different bones. Bones are of three types: long bones, as in the limbs; short bones, as in the wrists; and flat bones, as in the skull. The bones are connected to each other at specialized areas called *joints,* or *articulations.*

Most, though not all, of the joints in the body allow for varying degrees of motion. The typical joint that permits motion consists of opposing bones whose surfaces are covered by a firm but pliant tissue called the *articular cartilage.* The end of each bone connected by the joint is covered by a layer of this cartilage, and its surface is smooth, glistening, and capable of sliding. The cartilage, in turn, is covered by a thin layer of cells called the *synovium,* which continues around the joint to form a closed sac called the *joint space.* This sac, or joint space, normally contains a small amount of lubricating fluid called the *synovial fluid.*

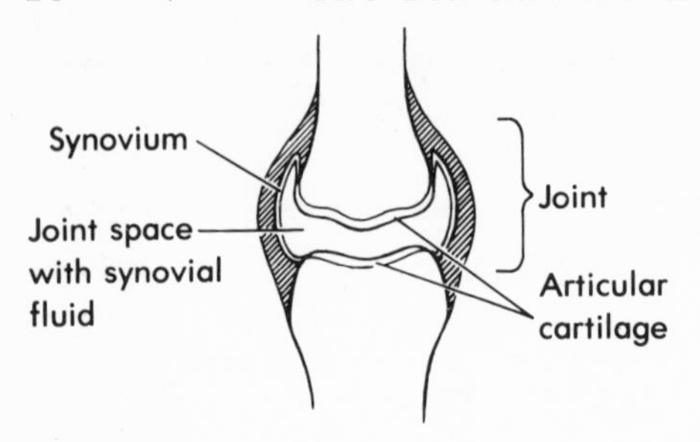

A simple joint

When we use the term *arthritis,* we are referring to a form of rheumatism that means inflammation of a joint. Such inflammation can stem from any one of many causes and can involve any part of the joint. If the cartilage is damaged or inflamed, this causes arthritis. Examples are osteoarthritis (also called degenerative arthritis) and traumatic arthritis (which is linked to physical injury). Some types of arthritis, such as rheumatoid arthritis or lupus erythematosus, begin with an inflammation of the synovium. Even the synovial fluid itself can become inflamed and cause arthritis, as in gout. Arthritis can be caused by infections, such as gonorrhea or tuberculosis. Temporary joint inflammations can occur with viral illnesses such as German measles or chicken pox.

Clearly, then, that form of rheumatism we call arthritis is an affliction of the joints. It is of equal importance to understand that in many cases of arthritis *other* tissues in the body may also be contributing to the pain. These tissues may also be involved in the *absence* of arthritis. This now brings us to the anatomy of those other tissues—the ones involved in *soft-tissue rheumatism.*

The Soft Tissues

The parts of the body that are involved in soft-tissue rheumatism are, as the name implies, soft tissues as opposed to the hard or bony tissues that make up our joints. The three types of soft tissues that we will be concerned with here are the connective tissues, cartilage, and skeletal muscles.

Connective tissues are specialized tissues that connect, or are interposed between, various other tissues and bones. There are several kinds of connective tissue: *Ligaments* and *joint capsules* support and stabilize the joints. *Fascias* give support and protection to muscles. *Tendons* connect certain muscles to bones, allowing us to move our bones and joints at will. *Bursas* are enclosed sacs that assist tissues in sliding over each other where our muscles and joints move.

Cartilage is a translucent elastic tissue that serves various functions. Its presence gives form and support, for example, to our ears and noses. It also connects ribs to the sternum (the breastbone). In addition, cartilage lines many joints; in this function it is called articular cartilage, described in the preceding section. As we noted there, damage to articular cartilage is considered to be a part of arthritis, since the cartilage lies within the joint.

The *skeletal muscles* are the third category of soft tissues. Although they contain small amounts of connective tissues, they are a distinct type of soft tissue.

Let's take a closer look at these three categories of soft tissue and, briefly, at how inflammation—tissues' reaction to injury—affects them.

Connective Tissue

Joint Capsules and Ligaments: Strictly speaking, the joint capsules and ligaments are considered by some anatomists to be parts of the joints. I have included them here because they are often involved with disease in the absence of arthritis.

A *joint capsule* is a dense band of connective tissue; it envelops the joint and attaches itself to both bones at the periphery of the joint surfaces. Basically, a joint capsule holds the joint together.

The *ligaments* are distinct from the joint capsules and are narrow bands of connective tissue that attach to the bony margins of the joint. The ligaments are essential to the mechanics of joint motion and assist in stabilizing the joints.

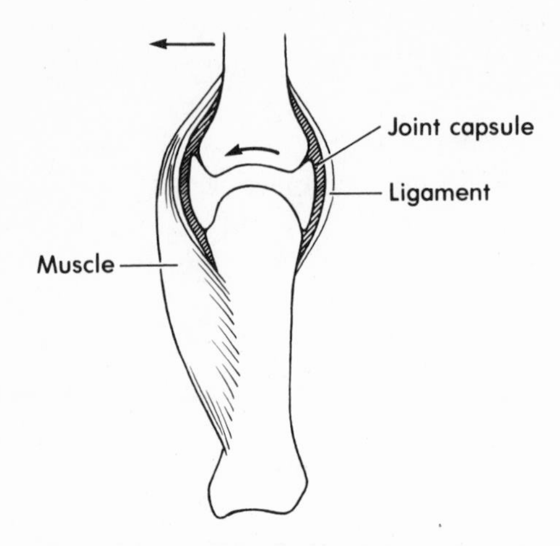

Joint capsule and surrounding structures

Most of the ligaments are on the outside of the joint, but some, such as the cruciate (cross-shaped) ligaments of the knee, are on the inside. Both the capsule and the ligaments of a joint can be damaged in various ways—through trauma or inflammation, for example. When these tissues are inflamed, we attach the suffix *-itis* and get the terms *capsulitis* and *ligamentitis*.

The joint capsules and ligaments are in very close proximity to the ends of the bones and the articular cartilage. Thus, any condition resulting in pain in these two soft-tissue structures might easily—though erroneously—be diagnosed as joint inflammation, or arthritis.

Tendons: Muscles can attach to bone directly, or they can attach by means of connective tissue—*tendons*—through which they exert their pull. Tendons are strong, glistening, cordlike structures that attach to a muscle at one end and a bone or joint at the other. Tendons often pass through structures called *tendon sheaths,* which assist in protecting and lubricating the tendons. Tendons are often worked pretty hard and can get inflamed and irritated, a condition known as—you guessed it—*tendinitis.* Those who follow the sports pages or the careers of musicians and ballet dancers are fa-

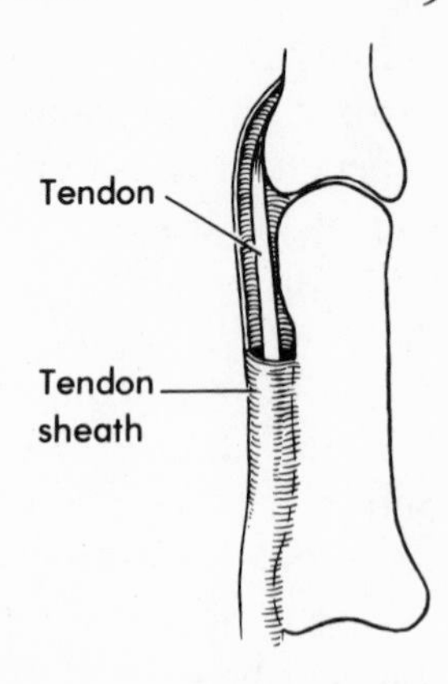

A tendon and tendon sheath

miliar with this term. Careers are often interrupted by episodes of tendinitis, which can result in considerable disability.

Fascias: The same type of tissue that makes up the cord-like tendons also forms flat sheets of tissue that protect easily damaged structures. This type of tissue is called a *fascia.* Fascias are found, for example, in the palm of the hand and the sole of the foot. Fascias give support and protection to

Plantar fascia

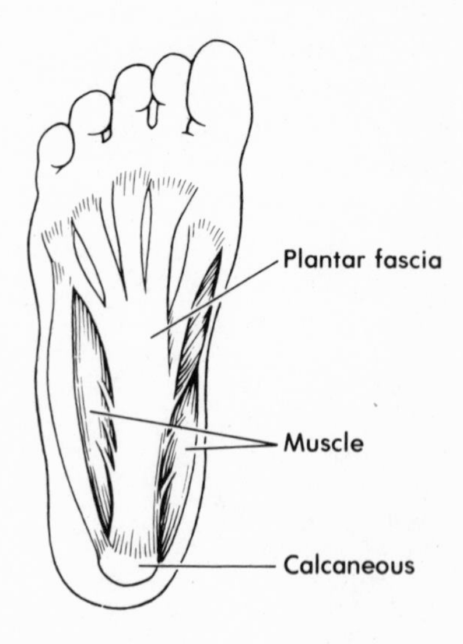

the muscles. In the hand, the fascias might be involved in a chronic type of inflammation that causes the ring and little fingers to contract or draw down. In the sole of the foot, one end of the fascia is attached to the heel, and inflammation here can cause a very painful heel. This problem is often known as "heel spurs," although most commonly no bony heel spurs are actually present. Inflammation produces what is called *fasciitis*. The medical term for heel spurs, for example, is plantar fasciitis.

Bursas: Another type of tissue is the *bursa*. A bursa is an enclosed sac that contains a small amount of lubricating fluid and can be located between two muscles, a muscle and tendon, two tendons, a tendon and bone, or a bone and the skin. The bursa's function is to allow these tissues to slide easily over each other with a minimum of friction, much in the way a bearing works. When the bursa becomes inflamed, the condition is called *bursitis*. Bursitis is very common in the shoulders, hips, and knees, and is usually linked to an underlying tendinitis.

Cartilage Cartilage is also found in parts of the body other than the joints. When cartilage *not* in a joint is inflamed, it is called *chondritis,* from the Greek word *chondros,* meaning cartilage. In soft-tissue rheumatism, the cartilage between the ribs and sternum, for example, can become inflamed; this condition is called *costochondritis*.

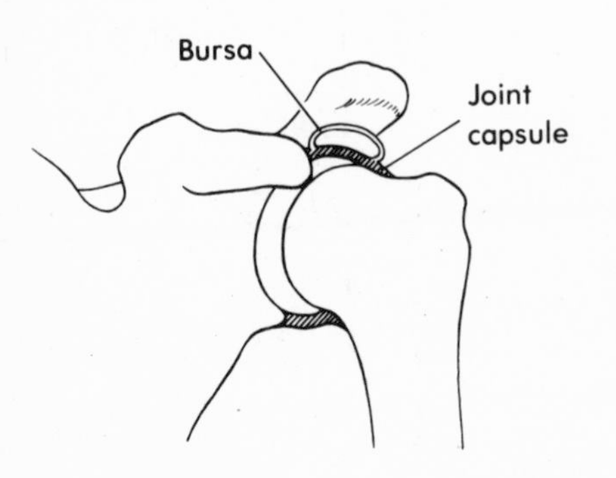

Shoulder bursa

Skeletal Muscles The skeletal muscles are specialized tissues that can contract and relax at your will, thus causing motion of the bones and joints. Each muscle is made up of many small muscle fibers of varying size.

Inflammation of the muscles is called *myositis.* Another important term is *myalgia:* aching or pain in the muscle *without* definite evidence of inflammation. One condition involving such pain is called polymyalgia rheumatica.

WHY? PAIN PERCEPTION AND RELIEF

Whenever we talk about rheumatism, one word comes to mind immediately: *pain.* Our battle is not only against rheumatism but also against the pain it gives.

Although we have all experienced it, pain is difficult to define in simple terms. In fact, many definitions are possible. For instance, in one view pain is any disagreeable sensation not associated with one of the special senses, such as taste, smell, or hearing. In another, pain is a perception, affection, or feeling resulting from a derangement of functions, bodily injury, or disease. Some hold that pain is an uneasiness of mind, such as grief. And still others relate pain to a punishment or penalty. In some circumstances pain is described as the state of being irked or annoyed or of experiencing suffering, distress, or displeasure. Clearly, the possible definitions of pain cover a wide spectrum, but central to all are

Cartilage involved in costochondritis

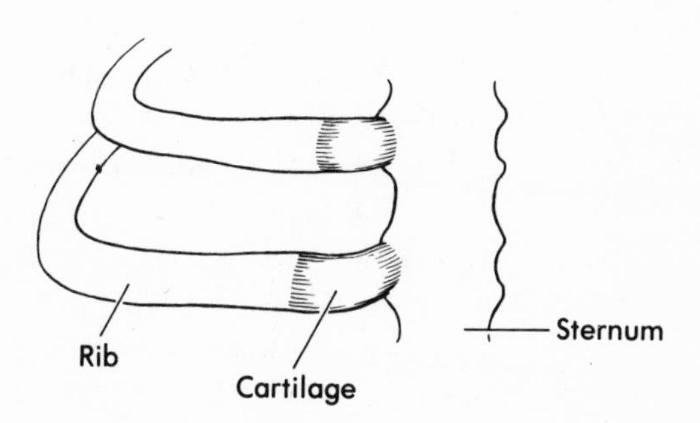

unpleasant perceptions—that is, an unpleasant conscious awareness. Because pain is a subjective experience, and because the word itself has such a wide variety of possible meanings, it is difficult both to understand the pain of others and to share our own.

A common misconception is to think of pain as originating exclusively from some form of physical injury to the tissues of our body (inflammation qualifies as injury here). In fact, pain can be generated in tissues of our body by brain signals and perceived via purely psychological mechanisms. The existence of pain is not dependent on tissue injury.

Another misconception is that pain can be relieved only by purely physical means, such as heat application, or chemical means, such as medication. If we held strictly to this line of reasoning, we would deprive ourselves of some extremely effective forms of pain reduction and relief. Diversions such as amusement and recreation, as examples, can often dramatically reduce the perception of pain. Humor is a time-honored method that directs attention away from many forms of discomfort.

You might think that logically there *should* be a direct relationship between the extent of injury present and the amount of pain perceived. Surprisingly, this is not always true. At times, injury and pain perception go their separate ways. Thus, it is possible to find little or no injury simultaneously with significant pain perception. Conversely, pain can occur *without* tissue injury or disease. The purely physical approach to understanding pain neglects major factors—our emotions and our psychological response systems.

The perception of pain involves a complex interaction between our bodies and minds—our soma and psyche. At times, as with the arthritic disease rheumatoid arthritis, the soma seems paramount. In certain forms of soft-tissue rheumatism, such as fibrositis and psychogenic rheumatism, the psyche assumes the major role.

It is impossible to overemphasize the soma-psyche interactions in an account of soft-tissue rheumatism pain. The importance of the interactions lies in the fact that there are many causes of pain and many pathways to pain relief. With this understanding, medical professionals are able to avoid or quickly abandon ineffective remedies. As we explore soma-psyche interactions, you will begin to grasp the reasons why it is best to treat not rheumatism itself, viewed as a disease, but a whole *person* who has rheumatism.

Injury and Pain

The statement that "injury can cause pain" is a truism. What is not as well appreciated is that injury and tissue damage can occur *without* pain and that, conversely, rheumatic and other pains can also occur *without* injury or tissue damage. Let's look at a few examples.

It has been well documented that many men who sustain severe battle wounds, even men who are alert and not in shock, initially complain of little or no pain. These same men might, however, complain bitterly of pain from the stick of a needle when they are given a blood transfusion. The most likely explanation for their lack of pain perception or sensation in their wounds is that the feelings of relief and elation for being allowed to leave the battlefield alive prevail over their perception of pain.

Another classic example of injury without pain is that of people who hear a shot and don't realize until they see the blood that it is they who have been wounded. In such a situation, their preoccupation with other matters overrules their perception of pain.

It is possible to have a considerable amount of arthritis and still have no pain. A typical case is that of an elderly man who is in an automobile accident and hurts his neck. An X-ray examination of the cervical spine ordered after the accident shows signs of severe osteoarthritis and disc degeneration even though the man had previously experienced no neck pain at all. These changes could have been going on for years—

and without pain. The important point is that it is often difficult to predict a person's symptoms simply by looking at an X ray. It's worth adding that if a person does have neck pain and an X ray shows arthritic changes, the pain is not always attributable to these changes.

Now let's look at the other side of the coin—pain without injury. The point here is that pain without injury is as real to the sufferer as the pain of a person with a detectable wound. (I am, of course, making a distinction here between true pain without injury and malingering.)

In many recorded instances, a person who has witnessed an injury has experienced the same pain as the injured party. Also, it is well known that mental depression can be associated with pains in various parts of the body, and that such pains disappear when the depression lifts. Muscle tension alone can cause pain. There is a simple way to convince yourself that this is true. Stand with your back to the wall and slide down until your thighs are perpendicular to the floor. Stay that way for a short time and you'll notice increasing discomfort in the thighs, followed by outright pain. This maneuver has been touted as an exercise for skiers. It's an exercise, all right—in pain tolerance.

An uncommon cause of pain is related to what is known as the thalamic stroke syndrome. If the specialized area of the brain called the thalamus is damaged by a stroke, the results can include the sensation of pain or burning on one side of the body. We know, therefore, that changes in the brain itself can result in the perception of pain in healthy areas of the body.

Another feature of pain is that it can persist long after an injury has healed or a disease has been cured. At least two very severe kinds of pains fall into this category. The first is "phantom limb pain," in which an amputee feels excruciating pains in the limb that has been removed. The second is "post-herpetic neuralgia," which follows an infection known as "shingles," or herpes zoster. A small percentage of people with shingles have pain that continues long after the infection has cleared up.

Now let's suppose that you're a researcher pursuing the cause and perception of pain. Your theories are going to have to explain the following categories of known experience:

Injury followed by pain
Injury without pain
Pain without injury
Pain long after an injury has healed

If you think you have a big job on your hands, let me add something else you'll have to explain. Your theories will have to tell us why such varied forms of treatment as medications, heat, cold, acupuncture, acupressure, and counter-irritation (such as the application of liniments or electrical stimulation) can be effective pain relievers. In addition, your theories will have to account for the fact that variations in our emotional states may increase or decrease our perception of pain!

Since much of this work has already been done for us, let's consider the three main categories of theories on pain perception—the neurological, biochemical, and psychological theories. They are not exclusive of one another, since one or more mechanisms often seem to play a part in pain perception.

Neurological Theories of Pain Perception The earliest neurophysiological theory of pain proposed that injury to specific "pain fibers" carried a message to a "pain center" in the brain. Presumably, some type of noxious or hurtful stimulation such as trauma or inflammation at the nerve endings would initiate the transmission of an electrical impulse to a specific area in the brain and be interpreted as pain. More complex theories evolved from this, but their basis is the same. Pain is considered to be transmitted to a pain center in the brain primarily in terms of electrical impulses.

No known nerve fibers, however, are specifically dedicated to carrying only "pain" impulses. Certain types of small nerve fibers are the primary carriers of the so-called pain sensations, but they also carry impulses that can be interpreted as other sensations, such as heat or cold. The dental drill, for example, causes vibration, heat, and pressure. One person may perceive these sensations as annoying and another as excruciating pain. It has been proven that stimulating certain types of nerve fibers can produce pain, while stimulating others can suppress it. Conditions in which pain persists long after an injury or disease is healed (for example, phantom limb pain and post-herpetic neuralgia) are considered to relate to imbalances in the nerve fibers that play a role in producing or suppressing pain. Depending on the type of stimulus to the nerve endings, and on the type of nerve endings that are stimulated, it should be possible either to increase or decrease the amount of pain a person perceives. These theories have led to exciting insights into why such devices as the transcutaneous electrical nerve stimulator and such treatments as liniments and acupuncture can give temporary pain relief. The transcutaneous electrical nerve stimulator (TENS) is a small battery-powered device that delivers pulsating low-intensity electrical shocks to the skin.

The Biochemical Theory of Pain Perception Another theory of pain production recognizes the part that biochemical changes play in our perception of pain. Initially, studies in this area were directed toward understanding the part that inflammation—produced by trauma or infection, for example—plays in producing noxious chemical substances such as histamines, kinins, prostaglandins, and serotonin. These substances are known to play important roles in both the process of inflammation and the production of pain. Through intensive research in the area we have gained a better understanding of the effects of anti-inflammatory drugs and other medications in combating pain.

One of the most exciting discoveries of the past decade has been the finding that morphine-like substances are naturally produced in the brain. There is evidence to suggest that these potent pain killers, called *enkephalins* and *endorphins,* can be produced by changes in emotional states. They may well help to explain why "mind control" may be effective in pain relief. The biochemical approach to pain perception, though relatively new, has already been effective in the design of new anti-inflammatory and analgesic medications.

The Psychological Theory of Pain A third theory of pain perception centers on its psychological aspects. Before the nineteenth century, pain was considered to be an emotion, like happiness or sadness. Later it was viewed more as a perception or sensation related to past and present experiences and future expectations. More recently, psychological researchers have suggested that pain may be more closely related to such feelings as hunger and thirst.

Despite our difficulty in defining the nature of pain, we are certain of the fact that pain perception can be produced or enhanced by such psychological states as depression and severe anxiety. We also know that exhilaration and distraction can suppress the perception of pain. A baseball player who finished a game despite a broken finger was asked whether it hurt much. He answered that it didn't hurt when you were winning.

The realization that our psychological and emotional responses can play a part in pain perception gives us other weapons to use in our fight against pain. By relieving anxiety, fear, hostility, and undesirable forms of stress, we can also reduce the perception of pain.

Choosing a Treatment

The various theories of pain production and perception are not mutually exclusive. It appears that all three kinds of mechanisms—neurological, biochemical, and psychological—participate simultaneously, and it may be difficult to identify which plays the greatest role in pain production and perception in any person at any given time. Since many factors are at play, it is often necessary to provide more than one form of therapy for the relief of pain. And, although ideally we treat both the *production* and *perception* of pain, we may not know its cause in a given real-life case. At times, therefore, treatment has to be "empirical." This means the therapy is based on practical experience; in other words, it works.

Although it's desirable to know exactly *why* something works, it's sometimes enough to know that it *does* work. For example, though we've been using drugs such as aspirin effectively since the end of the nineteenth century, we're still trying to figure out exactly how they work. I don't mean to imply that little is known about the mechanisms of pain relief; this would be untrue and an insult to the many investigators who have taught us much about why medications and the other methods are effective. There is still a lot to learn, however, and the final chapter is far from written.

Many factors cause pain, and many factors are involved in the perception of pain and its relief. You will learn more about our individual responses to the interplay of these factors and how our responses to pain can be the determining factor in *function* versus *disability* in the soft-tissue rheumatic diseases. You will also come to understand more about why it is necessary to treat not the rheumatic process alone but the whole person as a complex being reacting to disease and injury.

WHAT? FORMS OF SOFT-TISSUE RHEUMATISM

As indicated earlier, what we call soft-tissue rheumatism actually consists of many diseases. We need a simple way of classifying these disorders based on the origins of the symptoms that accompany them. One approach is to consider the kind of discomfort these diseases produce—whether localized or diffuse. The *localized disorders* cause pain in one specific area. They are literally disorders that you can "put your finger on." The *diffuse disorders* cause more widespread and often more vague pains in one or more areas of the body. Thus, we have two major categories: localized and diffuse forms of soft-tissue rheumatism. If you have soft-tissue rheumatism and can point to your pain with a finger, you probably have one of the localized disorders listed below. If the area of pain is more widespread, and particularly if it involves both sides of your body, you probably have one of the diffuse disorders. These are not hard-and-fast rules by any means; they are intended only as guidelines.

Here is a breakdown of the disorders we will consider.

LOCALIZED	DIFFUSE
Tendinitis	Fibrositis
Bursitis	Psychogenic rheumatism
Capsulitis	Polymyalgia rheumatica
Ligamentitis	Giant cell arteritis
Fasciitis	Reflex sympathetic dystrophies
Costochondritis	
Nerve entrapment syndromes	

THE LOCALIZED FORMS

Tendinitis: Tendons and their sheaths can become inflamed anywhere along their length. Pressure, motion, or a pull on inflamed tendons will increase pain. Common areas of involvement are shoulders, elbows, wrists, fingers, hips, knees, ankles, and feet.

Bursitis: Bursal inflammations are most often secondary to adjacent tendinitis. Pressure on or motion involving the bursa increases pain. Common areas of involvement are the shoulders, hips, and knees.

Capsulitis: Inflammation of the joint capsule usually results in severely restricted joint motion and considerable pain. The most common form of involvement is that of the shoulder joint.

Ligamentitis: The pain of ligament inflammation is most

apparent when the ligament is stressed by joint motion. The knee and ankle are most commonly involved.

Fasciitis: Inflammation can occur anywhere in the fascia but is most likely to occur at the point where it attaches to a bone. The most common form is plantar fasciitis, which is generally known as a "heel spur." Fascias are found in various areas, including the neck, back, thigh, hands, and feet.

Costochondritis: In certain areas of the body, cartilage that is separate from joints can become inflamed. The cartilage inflammation that can occur in soft-tissue rheumatism most commonly involves that which lies between the ribs and the sternum. The pain that results is often erroneously thought to be coming from the heart.

Nerve Entrapment Syndromes: In various parts of the body, ligaments are in close proximity to nerves. If the ligament is swollen or in any way inflamed, it can put pressure on the adjacent nerve. The result can be pain, tingling, or numbness in the area that the nerve supplies with sensory endings. The most common forms cause these symptoms in the wrist, hand, and fingers (carpal tunnel syndrome) or in the upper and outside part of the thigh (meralgia paresthetica).

The Diffuse Forms

Fibrositis: This condition primarily affects women in their twenties and thirties and around the time of menopause, but it is certainly not restricted to women of these ages or to women in particular. Fibrositis is characterized by the aching and stiffness of muscles that is often made worse by cold. Associated symptoms may include tingling, numbness, feelings of joint swelling, fatigue, anxiety, and depression. Despite the many symptoms accompanying fibrositis, there has never been a single abnormal laboratory study or X-ray finding that would give a clue as to its cause. Many sufferers are erroneously thought to have any one of a number of other disorders, most often rheumatoid arthritis. Its cause is rooted in the close relationship between body and mind—soma and psyche.

Psychogenic Rheumatism: This is a specific form of rheumatism in which pain is perceived in areas of the body that are perfectly normal. As the name implies, the disease is entirely of psychological origin and is related to what are known as "psychological conversion reactions" rather than to true rheumatism.

Polymyalgia Rheumatica: This disease rarely occurs in people younger than fifty years of age, and its frequency increases with age. It is characterized by severe stiffness and often pain in the shoulder and hip areas. It may appear suddenly or progress slowly; in both cases it can result in severe immobility and disability. The symptoms and pathology of this disorder blend into those of giant cell arteritis.

Giant Cell Arteritis: This disorder has the same age distribution as polymyalgia rheumatica. The symptoms may be the same as those of polymyalgia rheumatica and may also include severe headaches, high fevers, weight loss, anemia, and blindness. The underlying cause is a poorly understood inflammation of blood vessels in various parts of the body.

Reflex Sympathetic Dystrophies: These disorders can occur after an injury to a limb or nerve ranging in intensity from trivial to severe, but they can also occur in the absence of any injury. They cause excruciating pain in a limb and associated tissue swelling, skin-temperature abnormalities, and perspiration in the affected area. One form, the shoulder-hand syndrome, can occur after a heart attack. Untreated, reflex sympathetic dystrophies can result in permanent disability of a limb.

I will discuss the localized forms of soft-tissue rheumatism as a group. Since tendinitis is the most common form of localized soft-tissue rheumatism, I refer to these disorders as "the tendinitis group." Also, since these disorders can strike many parts of the body, the clearest approach is to describe them in terms of areas of the body, and the types of disorders most likely to occur at each site.

I will discuss the diffuse forms of soft-tissue rheumatism separately. The exceptions are polymyalgia rheumatica and giant cell arteritis. Since these two diseases often blend, I will describe them together.

3

Putting Your Finger on the Pain: The Tendinitis Group

HOW THE DIAGNOSIS IS MADE

How do you or your doctor know that you have tendinitis or one of the other localized disorders?

Recall that tendons are strong, cordlike tissues that attach muscles to bones or joints. Inflammation of tendons, called tendinitis, is the most common form of the localized soft-tissue rheumatic disorders. The other conditions in this group are bursitis, capsulitis, ligamentitis, fasciitis, costochondritis, and nerve entrapment syndromes. All the tissues affected in this group—the tendons, ligaments, joint capsules, and fascias—are similar in their composition and in the problems that affect them. Further, bursas—the bearing-like sacs that lie between muscles, tendons, and the like—can become inflamed themselves or be secondarily involved. This may be due to their close proximity to an inflamed tendon or ligament.

In the tendinitis group, inflammation affects not just tendons but ligaments, joint capsules, fascias, and bursas as well. The nerve entrapment syndromes, however, differ in their cause. They result when a nerve is compressed, for instance by a ligament, causing various combinations of tingling, numbness, and pain along the course of the nerve.

When one of the soft tissues is irritated, pain occurs in a specific area. With a knowledge of anatomy, one can press down with a fingertip and cause the pain to increase. It takes a little experience to do this correctly as a diagnostic technique. There are also various ways of stretching and putting tension on tendons and other tissues to ascertain that inflammation is present.

Knowing the location of the pain alone will allow you to make an educated guess as to the cause, but a true diagnosis is based on a careful history and physical examination. Laboratory studies are of little value in diagnosing tendinitis, since they are usually normal whether or not inflammation is present. X-ray examinations can help some, since there may be calcium deposits in the inflamed area. But the presence of calcium only suggests that inflammation has been present in the past; it doesn't tell the entire story about the present. Also, if two structures, such as a ligament and joint capsule, are near each other, it may be difficult to pinpoint the problem as one or both. Again, various types of examination help in making such distinctions.

WHY IT HAPPENS

Tendons and similar tissues can become irritated and inflamed in various ways. Injury is one way; excessive use is another. However, what constitutes excessive use varies among people according to the tolerance of their tissues. Every material on earth—be it cloth, wood, metal, plastic, glass, or animal or human tissue—will begin to show signs of wear at some point. Inanimate materials begin to crack or tear, and living tissue develops stress or inflammatory responses that result in pain or discomfort. Excessive use of muscles and tendons—and their improper use as well—predisposes us to this inflammatory reaction. As you will recall, inflammation is tissue response to injury, and it results in various degrees of localized heat, redness, swelling, and pain. Excessive use of tendons has long been recognized as a cause of tendinitis, and the names given to these painful conditions reflect the many occupations and diversions that are affected. To name a few, we have:

- Athlete's pubic pain
- Ballet foot
- Dancer's hip
- Espresso wrist
- Golfer's elbow
- Housemaid's knee
- Jumper's knee
- Musician's hand
- Nun's knee
- Overuse syndrome in athletes
- Pac-man tendinitis
- Pipesetter's shoulder
- Rug cutter's knee
- Shopping bag syndrome
- Slot machine tendinitis
- Soldier's heel
- Tennis elbow
- Wall washer's thumb
- Washerwoman's sprain
- Weaver's bottom
- Welder's shoulder

Infection—that is, the presence in the body of damaging microorganisms—is another cause of tendinitis. One of the most common infections in this regard is gonorrhea. The disease is not a major cause of tendinitis but, as discussed in a later section, is a possible diagnosis where fever accompanies localized pain.

Genetic predisposition may be another cause of tendinitis. This means that something in an individual's genetic background makes his or her tissues particularly susceptible to inflammation. The notion that heredity plays a role in tendinitis is as yet only a theory based on the observation of families. Genetic predisposition to certain forms of arthritis is an accepted fact, but the same situation is yet to be proven in tendinitis.

Tendinitis is also associated with certain arthritic diseases, such as rheumatoid arthritis, ankylosing spondylitis, the arthritis associated with psoriasis, and a condition known as Reiter's disease. Though we will not discuss these diseases in detail, I mention them for general information.

Tendinitis and the other localized forms of connective tissue inflammation are due to localized abnormalities of the tissues brought on by trauma, stress, overuse, improper use, infection, an associated arthritic condition, or possibly a genetic predisposition. The result is pain and tenderness over the affected area. To make an accurate diagnosis, the examining doctor takes a careful medical history and performs a physical examination. Laboratory tests and X rays are inconclusive in cases of tendinitis.

AREAS OF INVOLVEMENT

Any tendon or connective tissue in the body has the capacity to become inflamed, but certain ones are more susceptible than others. Inflammation seems to occur in most cases after unusual stress, motion, or trauma to the tissues. The most frequently involved areas are those where these three factors are present together. We are not, unfortunately, born with 40,000-mile guarantees on our tendons. Let's look at the areas most likely to be affected.

The Shoulder

The shoulder joint is a "ball and socket" joint. The head of the humerus (the upper arm bone) is shaped like a ball at the top and fits into a socket, which is part of the scapular bone. This arrangement allows for a wide range of motion. Consequently, the surrounding tissues are subject to much wear and tear that may result in inflammation and pain. Four types of soft tissues in the shoulder area can cause a lot of trouble. They are the

- tendons in the area of the joint capsule
- bursa
- long head of the biceps tendon
- joint capsule itself.

Let's begin with the tendons in the area of the joint capsule. Inflammation here produces pain in the upper part of the shoulder or in the muscle on the upper and outer part of

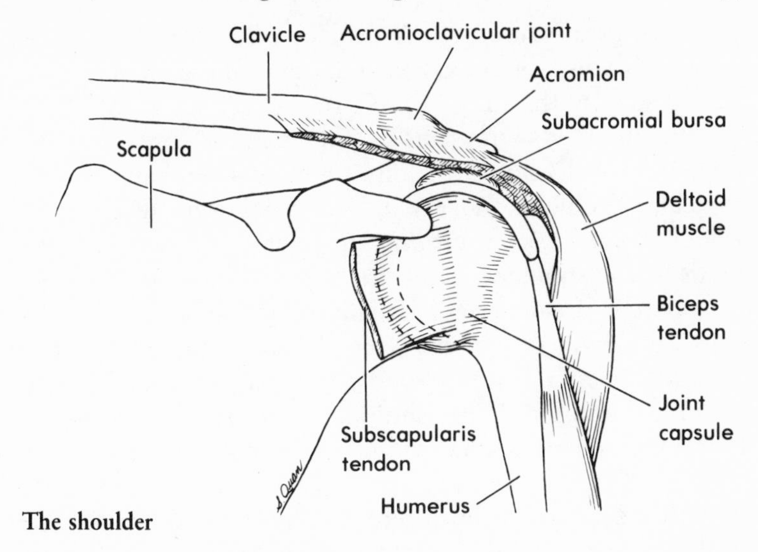

The shoulder

the arm (the deltoid muscle). In fact, many people with shoulder problems feel pain only in the deltoid area when they move their shoulder. This is called *referred* pain. When the shoulder is moved, the pain grows worse. It can be mild or so severe that it is intolerable even at rest. People often show up at my office with slings on their arms and tears in their eyes. An X-ray examination of the shoulder is often helpful in pinpointing the area of trouble, since calcium deposits might be visible. This condition has been given many names; if you have it, your doctor may call it *peritendinitis, calcific tendinitis,* or *bursitis.*

The word *bursitis,* though commonly used, doesn't tell the whole story. There is no question that the bursa can become inflamed, but where this happens the usual cause is inflammation of adjacent tissues, which apparently sets off the same process in the bursa. Bursal inflammation—at the end of the elbow, for instance—can be painless if adjacent tissues are not involved. Thus, even if the bursas in your shoulder are inflamed, it is likely that the surrounding tissues are the original source of the problem. But don't feel guilty if you call your shoulder pain bursitis. The name has been around so long that most people recognize it.

The shoulder's joint capsule—the band of connective tissue that basically holds the joint together—can have its own particular problems. A very painful condition called *frozen shoulder,* or *adhesive capsulitis,* frequently confused with tendinitis of the shoulder, can arise after a minor injury or for no apparent reason at all. Usually only one shoulder is affected, but both can be involved. I recall one woman who was driving on a country road and struck a deer. She saw the animal and tensed her shoulders a second before she hit it. The next day, both her shoulders were so tender that she was truly in a state of misery.

Other cases erupt in different ways. Let's say you can't recall injuring your left shoulder, but suspect that you may have "pulled a muscle" the night before. What starts out as a mild discomfort ends up that evening as an excruciatingly severe pain that totally restricts your shoulder motion. You're unable to sleep, even with the help of a few aspirin and codeine tablets that you have in the house. Hoping that it will just go away, you try some heat and then ice packs. The pain gets worse. You've heard about rheumatoid arthritis—maybe this is it. You make an urgent trip to your physician and get an X-ray examination of the shoulder, which proves to be normal. Your blood tests show no evidence to suggest inflammation. Your doctor injects the shoulder and you feel no better. The shoulder is totally disabled. Arthritis? Bursitis of the shoulder?—no. You have a condition known as "frozen shoulder" or "adhesive capsulitis." Your physician explains the differences and reassures you that although you will have a period of pain requiring treatment with medications and exercise, the outlook for relief is excellent.

Frozen shoulder and tendinitis differ markedly in their courses and treatments. The pain and disability of frozen shoulder long outlast those of tendinitis. For the former, the first line of therapy is to reduce the pain, which usually requires that some strong painkillers be administered for days or even months. Injections of cortisone derivatives can be tried, though they usually don't help very much. After the pain has been reduced, physical therapy is used to improve the range of shoulder motion. It will improve slowly under a course of therapy, and in nearly all cases a full range of motion is restored within a year. So if you ever have a frozen shoulder, take heart—it *will* get better.

While we're in the vicinity of the shoulder, I want to mention another condition that can mimic tendinitis: arthritis of the acromioclavicular joint. This joint is where the collarbone meets the shoulder. If you're thin, you can probably feel the joint easily. The ligaments and joints here are often damaged by sports injuries. The joint capsule can be injured and may actually be torn. This condition is not really "rheumatism," but I mention it to complete the picture.

An inch or two down from the shoulder lies the long head of the biceps muscle (the muscle popularized by the comic strip character Popeye). The tendon above the biceps travels over a groove in the humerus (the bone in the upper part of the arm). Inflammation can occur here and can be easily confused with tendinitis closer to the shoulder. This condition has the very impressive name of *bicipital tenosynovitis*.

We see that the shoulder is a beautifully designed joint, but it is not free of flaws given its susceptibility to various forms of soft-tissue rheumatism. As you might suspect, to treat these problems properly, the diagnosis has to be correct. Good treatments are available, and we'll get to them after looking at some other areas of tendinitis.

The Elbow

The elbow is a frequent target of tendinitis and serves as a perfect example of how one person's nuisance can be another's catastrophe. This seemingly simple joint is really a combination of two joints. One allows the forearm to bend back and forth on the arm; the other moves as you turn your hand and forearm back and forth. Both of these joints permit independent motion, which you can feel easily with your opposite hand as you move the elbow and cause motion between the humerus and ulna, and the radius and ulna. At the end of the humerus are little protuberances called *epicondyles.* One is located medially (toward the middle of the body) and the other laterally (toward the other side). Muscles from the forearm attach at both of these areas and can undergo quite a bit of stress if the arm is used much. And, as noted earlier, a lot of stress can cause inflammation.

You have probably heard of "tennis elbow," which is a popular name for *lateral epicondylitis.* It's more common than "golfer's elbow," which is a *medial epicondylitis.* Both are often referred to as tennis elbow, but it is useful to differentiate between them. Pain in these areas is by no means restricted to tennis players and golfers, and even mild overuse can cause inflammation and pain. The ligament that holds the radius to the ulna can also be a source of trouble.

What clues suggest the presence of a tennis or golfer's elbow? Your first hint will be pain in either of these areas after such simple motions as picking up a glass, lifting a light load, opening a door, or even shaking hands. If the inflam-

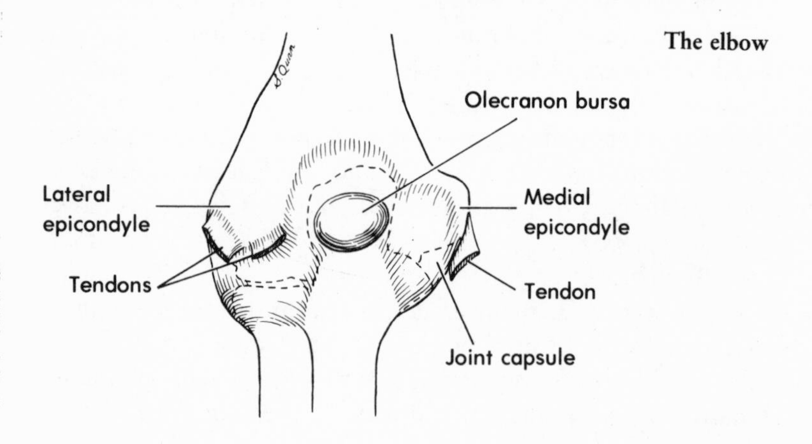

The elbow

mation is mild, it may take a stronger strain to cause the pain, such as hitting a ball with a tennis racket. The pain involved can range from a simple annoyance to the disabling of your forearm. Should your livelihood depend on frequent use of the forearm and elbow, you could be out of a job until the problem is resolved. Fortunately, as I'll make clear later, these inflammations usually respond very well to treatment.

Diagnosing tendinitis in the elbow is usually quite easy. A few maneuvers put stress on these areas and bring out the pain. However, if you have a disorder such as rheumatoid arthritis *plus* tennis or golf elbow, a doctor can easily misinterpret the pain as an arthritic one. I saw one such patient whose arthritis was in a state of remission, except for pain in one elbow. She had tried every medication in the book before coming to the office. The problem was easily solved with a small injection into the tender area. Tennis elbow is very common, and hardly a week goes by without my seeing a few patients with this disorder.

A special word of caution is in order for young athletes and their parents. Little League pitchers and budding golf pros can develop a special problem. The ends of the bones don't mature until the late teens, and before then pain can arise from damage to the bones in the area of the elbow joints. The symptoms may start out like a golfer's or tennis elbow but can be more serious. Don't let this situation go unattended in your child. I recommend a visit with an orthopedic surgeon at the first sign of discomfort.

Before leaving the elbow, I should mention the big bursa you rest your elbow on. It lies between the bone and the skin and sometimes takes quite a beating. It responds by swelling with fluid. There is usually no pain involved unless it becomes infected. An uninfected *olecranon bursitis* is more of a cosmetic nuisance than anything else and can improve spontaneously or respond to an injection. This bursa is commonly involved in rheumatoid arthritis and in such cases is not as responsive to treatment.

The Wrist and Hand

The wrist and hand are capable of providing infinite combinations of movements and are composed of many joints, ligaments, joint capsules, tendons, fascias, and muscles. Many of the tendons originate in the forearm and have to cross over the wrist to reach the fingers. As you might suspect, this complex system is subject to many stresses and strains. Any of these structures can become inflamed, but some areas are more frequently involved than others.

To find the site of one of the common problems, put your thumb in a position that you would use if you were hitchhiking. At the side of the wrist just below the thumb, you'll feel two tendons with a little hollow in between. That little hollow is called the "anatomical snuff box"; it had a lot of use when snuff was popular. The tendon closest to the palm can become inflamed, a condition with the rather overbearing name of *De Quervain's tenosynovitis*. Certain movements of the thumb and wrist can be quite painful where this condition

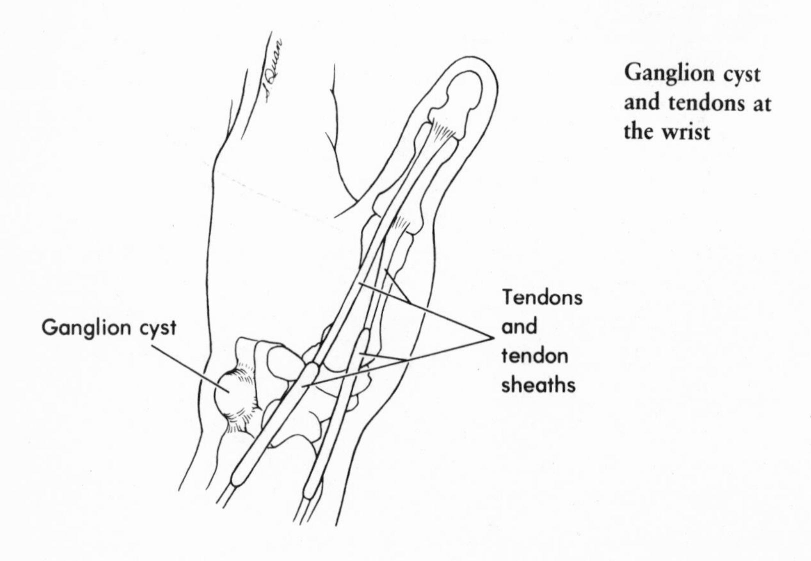

Ganglion cyst and tendons at the wrist

is present, and in some cases the tendon can become warm and swollen. De Quervain's tenosynovitis is sometimes confused with arthritis at the base of the thumb, but the difference is easily detectable. Any other tendon at the wrist can be affected, but that occurs less frequently.

Another source of wrist pain stems from a *ganglion cyst.* This is a swelling found on top of the wrist. If the cyst is small and not easily visible, arthritis may be erroneously suspected. You may have heard of this condition under the name of "Bible cyst," so named because it may disappear if you hit it with a Bible. You can do the same thing with any book, but the Bible obviously carries more authority! That technique is pretty outmoded anyway and can cause more pain than the cyst itself. An injection is more effective and not as uncomfortable. Save your Bible for reading.

The median nerve and carpal ligament

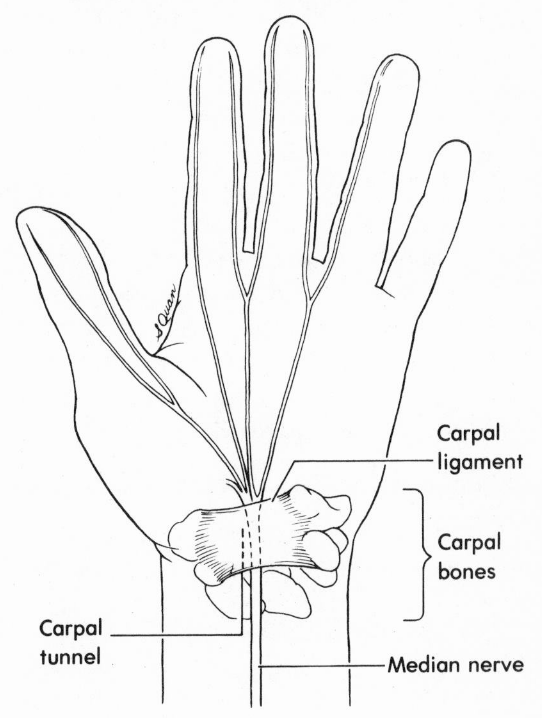

Carpal tunnel syndrome, or *median nerve compression,* is a common problem that begins in the wrist but is first noticed in the hand. The symptoms can be any combination of pain, numbness, and tingling in the thumb, index, middle, and/or ring fingers, plus possible pain radiating up the forearm. These symptoms are caused by a compression of the median nerve, usually by the carpal ligament. The median nerve runs across the palm side of the wrist under the carpal ligament, and the space it traverses is called the carpal tunnel. Any swelling of the ligament or other problem that narrows the tunnel causes pressure on the nerve, which results in the symptoms. The pain and tingling are typically worse at night and when the hands are held upright, as in driving a car. Rubbing or shaking the hand brings some temporary relief.

If you suspect that you might have the carpal tunnel syndrome, note carefully whether the symptoms occur in the little finger and the adjacent half of the ring finger. These areas are supplied by the ulnar nerve and should *not* be involved in a pure carpal tunnel (median nerve compression) syndrome. Confirmation of median nerve compression can be made by a test called "nerve conduction time," which measures the speed of the nerve impulse. A "positive" test will show a slowing of the nerve impulse where the compression occurs. Treatment can be rest and splinting, an injection in the ligament, or a surgical procedure that removes part of the ligament. The symptoms often respond to rest, and surgery is unnecessary. It's important not to attribute the symptoms to arthritis and to recognize the problem before the occurrence of permanent nerve damage, which can cause numbness and muscle wasting in the hand. I might add that certain conditions can predispose you to the carpal tunnel syndrome, such as rheumatoid arthritis, diabetes mellitus, and low thyroid function, though in most cases these underlying conditions are not present. Fortunately, carpal tunnel syndrome is a curable disorder, and those treated for it usually experience little or no residual disability after the necessary treatment.

We use our hands so much that it isn't surprising the tendons of the hands are often affected by tendinitis. The major sets of tendons are those that enable us to straighten and curl our fingers. Any of these tendons are subject to inflammation and can be painful indeed. Over the years I've seen countless musicians, hairdressers, housewives, potters, butchers, laborers—in short, people from all walks of life—with complaints of pain or "triggering" when they move their fingers. The most common areas of tendon inflammation are on the palmar side of the hand just before the knuckle joint where the fingers attach to the palm. Tendinitis here can be so painful it prevents the finger from bending at all. Any pressure on this area can lead to considerable discomfort. One or more tendons can be involved, and the painful area can extend into the finger, causing swelling and tightness that accentuate the pain.

Trigger finger is a finger that locks when it is flexed. It can actually give off a "snapping" feeling or sound when it is straightened. At times the finger locks so tightly you may have to use your other hand to pry it open. This condition is caused either by an inflammation in the tendon sheath that prevents it from sliding smoothly or by a little degenerative cyst that forms on the tendon. Pain is often present along with the "snapping" of the finger. Sometimes you can feel a tender nodule on the tendon at the area where the finger begins. In some instances the problem may go away by itself, or it may go away and come back. Treatment is that of the other types of tendinitis and will be discussed at the end of this chapter.

A condition affecting more men than women is a difficulty in straightening the ring and little fingers in one or both hands. This is due to *Dupuytren's contracture,* which is caused by a fibrosis or scarring of the fascia that lies under the skin of

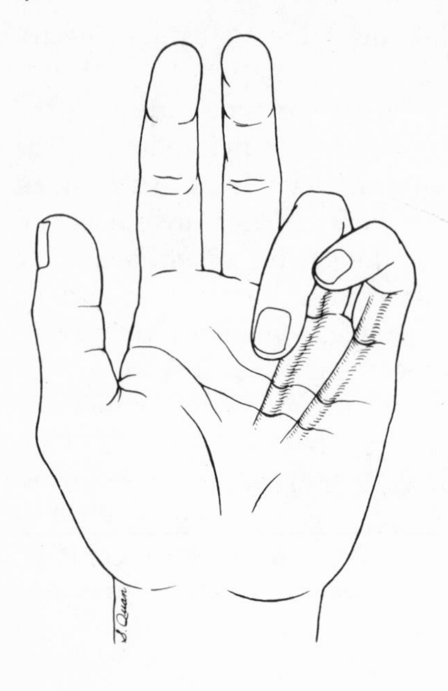

Dupuytren's contracture

the palm. It is usually painless. The scarring can cause only a slight thickening feeling in the palm or can progress to a point at which the ring and little fingers are permanently curled on the palm. Trauma may play a part in this condition, but I suspect that heredity plays a greater role. Dupuytren's contracture becomes a problem when the curling of the fingers is severe enough to interfere with the function of the hand. In mild cases, heat and stretching exercises may be of value in preventing deformity. If the situation progresses, injections in the area or even surgery may be needed. However, the condition can progress despite any form of therapy, and in this case it is better to be philosophical about the matter.

The Hip Area

Pain in the hip area can have many sources, including the joint, the surrounding tissues, and referral from the spine. The commonest cause in my practice comes from a well-known version of tendinitis known as *trochanteric bursitis.*

The hip joint, like the shoulder joint, is a ball-and-socket joint. There is a protuberance on the upper end of the femur (the thigh bone) called the *greater trochanter.* Just above this is the neck of the femur and then the head of the femur (the "ball" portion of the joint). Muscles from the buttocks attach at the greater trochanter. The *trochanteric bursa* overlies this attachment. When the tendon attachments to the greater trochanter are inflamed, the condition is known as trochanteric bursitis.

The typical story is that the "hip" begins to hurt as you walk up and down the stairs and often when you get up from a chair. At times the pain might inhibit you from lying on your side, thus interrupting your sleep. The discomfort can radiate down the outside of the thigh to the knee. As with other tendinitis problems, the pain may be mild or so severe that walking becomes almost impossible. There are a lot of variations on this theme. I recall a fifty-five-year-old businessman who had so much pain in the morning he had to stand on the painless leg and rest his arm on the sink to shave. Within an hour the pain would leave, only to return the next

The hip

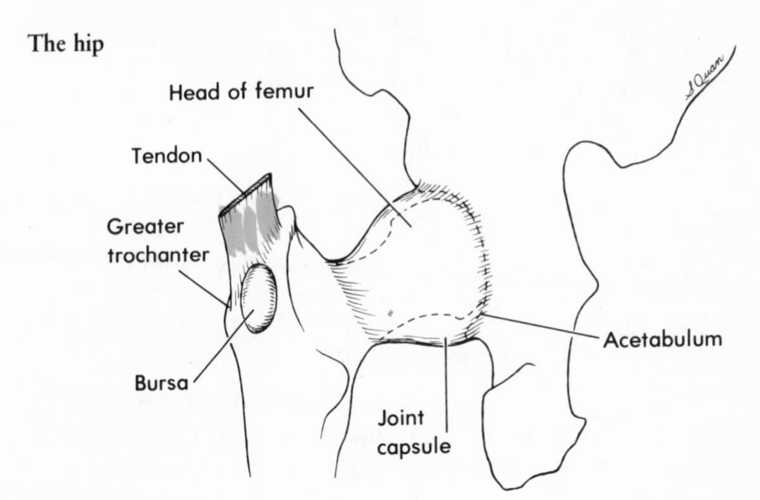

morning. Another patient, a forty-eight-year-old real estate salesman, climbed a long hill during a fishing trip. The next morning he had pain on the side of the hip that was so severe he had to be hospitalized. In many patients the pain comes and goes with neither rhyme nor reason. It is not unusual to have pain in both hips at the same time. Trochanteric bursitis can accompany or be easily confused with pain from arthritis of the hip or from sciatica, which occurs from a "pinched nerve" in the spine. Youth is no great barrier to trochanteric bursitis—even people in their twenties have it occasionally.

When the leg is out straight, the greater trochanter is covered by muscle, and it is very difficult to put your finger on the tender area. To best find this spot it is necessary to lie on the side that does not hurt, flex the affected hip to the chest, and push in around where the tendons insert. This technique requires some experience and may be difficult to do by yourself. An X-ray examination of the hip area is usually normal, or it may show a small amount of calcium deposit near the greater trochanter.

The Knee

Few areas in the body are subjected to as much stress as the knee and its surrounding and supporting tissues. One reason is that the knee has a wide range of motion, and it not only flexes and extends (bends and straightens) but has to withstand forces that put a twisting motion on it.

Let's consider just what this joint is expected to undergo. The knee gets a good workout when we walk, kneel, squat, run, bicycle, ski, jump, dance—you name it. In addition, it takes quite a beating in sports such as soccer, football, tennis, baseball, and the like. Other areas of the body may take a pounding too, but few have to tolerate it while supporting the weight of the body through such a range of motion. The knee is a vulnerable area, and therefore nature has given us the kneecap to help protect it from damage and has supplied

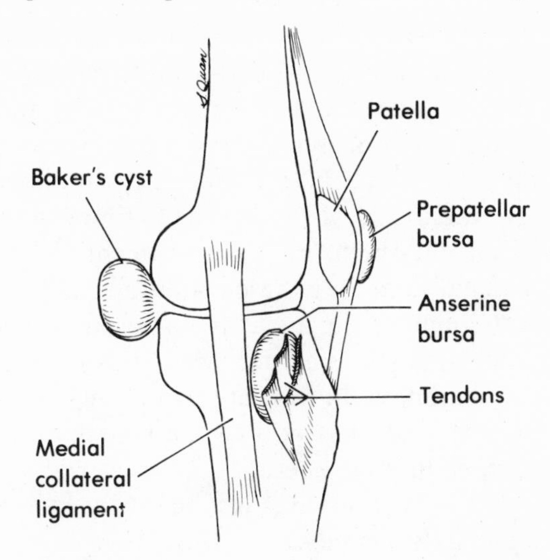

The knee

it with many ligaments and more bursas than any other part of the body.

Human nature being what it is, we all have a tendency to push this structural design to its limit—and beyond. In addition to arthritis and cartilage tears from trauma, the tissues surrounding the knee often respond to this stress by becoming inflamed and painful.

The patella, or *kneecap,* has a tendon attached to it on the top, a ligament on the bottom, and a big bursa between it and the overlying skin. Any of these three can become inflamed or irritated. The bursa over the kneecap can be easily damaged and may swell without causing pain, like the bursa at the elbow. Kneeling a lot is often the cause of such swelling, and the condition is seen frequently in carpet layers and nuns, for example. This swelling is referred to as *housemaid's knee,* but you obviously don't have to be a housemaid to get it.

There is a ligament on the inner aspect side of the knee called the *medial collateral ligament.* This ligament can become painful and is often confused with arthritis or a torn cartilage in the knee. All three are common occurrences, and it is not always easy to differentiate among them. Special studies might be needed—an arthrogram (an X ray taken after a radio-opaque dye is injected into the knee), for example, or arthroscopy (looking into the knee through an arthroscope, a tubular instrument that allows a surgeon to see into the inside of the knee). At times, with a small injection of an anesthetic into the ligament, a physician can easily distinguish among these conditions. Inflammation of the medial collateral ligament is not usually associated with knee swelling, so where knee swelling is present it's probably *not* just tendinitis. In fact, any knee swelling except housemaid's knee should alert you to the fact that you may have some damage in your knee.

I consider one area just below the knee a sort of "sleeper"; it is rarely diagnosed as the source of pain and, when pain exists there, the diagnosis is often erroneously thought to be arthritis of the knee. This spot is about one inch below the actual knee joint and about one inch in from the midline of the knee. The tendons of three muscles attach there and, not uncommonly, they are affected by tendinitis. There's also a bursa there called the *anserine bursa.* Often, although the problem is tendinitis, the poor bursa gets the blame and the pain is said to be due to *anserine bursitis.* Whatever you want to call it, it can be painful enough to cause you to limp. I recall one woman who believed for three years that she had arthritis of the knee. She was cured of her "arthritis" by a very small injection into the anserine area.

Before we leave the knee, a few words about *Baker's cyst* are in order. This cyst is named after Dr. William Morrant Baker and not your friendly bread man. It is also known by the name *popliteal cyst.* This is a swelling behind the knee in what is called the *popliteal fossa* and is caused by fluid in one or more bursas in this location. There are many causes for Baker's cyst, and practically every instance that I have seen is due to some problem within the knee joint. The "cysts" themselves are usually not painful. They may sometimes rupture, and fluid may be forced into the calf muscles. The swelling then appears in the calf and can be easily confused with a thrombophlebitis (a clot in the vein). The two conditions are differentiated by means of certain X-ray techniques.

SHIN SPLINTS

The term *shin splints* refers to pain in the shin, or the front part of the leg below the knee. They may follow long hours of walking or a lot of running. If you're an athlete, you're probably familiar with them. If you don't know what causes them, don't feel too badly—they are a source of controversy among medical authorities in sports medicine. I'm including them because one of their causes is thought to be tendinitis.

Typically, shin splints consist of a dull aching pain in the front and side part of the leg below the knee after strenuous activity such as running, playing basketball, or the like. When the discomfort is mild, it usually responds to rest. If activity is continued, the pain can get worse, even becoming chronic and disabling.

Experts in the field now believe that there are a few different causes for shin splints. There is also agreement that they usually occur when the leg is stressed without prior muscle conditioning. One of the causes is undoubtedly a tendinitis that results from overly stressing the tendons in this area and is similar to the forms of tendinitis we have already discussed. Other causes may be small stress fractures of the lower portions of the tibia or fibula. These fractures can be so small that they remain undetected in the usual X-ray examination. Another cause may be irritation of the cells covering the bone at the muscle attachments, a condition called *periostitis*. Yet another cause is swelling of the muscles. These leg muscles are in a tight compartment of connective tissue and when swollen become constricted and painful.

Most shin splint problems are mild, and a good athletic coach will treat them by rest followed by the gradual reconditioning of the muscles and tendons. The trick is really to prevent them by avoiding sudden and severe stresses of muscles and other tissues that have not been properly conditioned.

If the pains are severe or persistent, it would be wisest to see a physician, since the problem may not be a simple one. Pain in the calf of the leg, for example, could indicate a muscle tear or a more serious situation, such as a blood clot in a vein (thrombophlebitis).

The Ankle and Foot

We'll consider the ankle and foot together since they are what you might call close relatives. Like the knee, they take their share of abuse and let you know when they've had too much.

In the past few years, the great resurgence of interest in physical fitness in this country has made people more aware of the beneficial effects of exercise. Of all the forms of exercise, none has had such a spectacular following as jogging and marathon racing. Unfortunately, the incidence of tendinitis has paralleled the increase in running, and one of the more prevalent problems is now *Achilles' tendinitis*. The Achilles tendon is that big cord that you can feel behind the ankle. It connects the calf muscle to the heel and is under stress when you get up on your toes or pull your foot up.

It is interesting to speculate whether it was this condition that was immortalized in Greek mythology. As you may recall, Achilles' mother, Thetis, had intended to make Achilles invulnerable by dipping him into the river Styx when he was born. She held him by his heel, however, and the water did not cover that area. He died when Paris shot an arrow that was guided by Apollo and struck him in the heel—his only vulnerable spot. The ancient Greeks were well known as runners, and I suspect that they had their share of Achilles' tendinitis. In fact, the word "marathon" commemorates the Greek runner who ran forty kilometers (about 25 miles) from Marathon to Athens in the year 490 B.C. to announce the victory over the Persians. But you don't have to run a marathon to get Achilles' tendinitis, and it seems that certain susceptible people will have this problem just from being on their feet a great deal.

The recognition and treatment of Achilles' tendinitis has gotten much publicity recently in the magazines devoted to runners and joggers. There probably isn't a serious runner who is unaware of this condition. One important aspect of the disorder has become its prevention, and we can learn a lot from the runners. If you observe experienced runners before a race, you'll notice that they "warm up" and do stretching exercises, which, for the Achilles tendon, consists of putting the foot flat and leaning forward with the leg. Another less obvious point is that these runners have prepared for the stress of the race by gradually increasing the distances they run. I have known several people who have run marathons after having trained on shorter distances, only to end up with a painful tendon.

Other tendons cross the ankle joint, as tendons do to the wrist, and many of these can also become inflamed and painful.

The heel

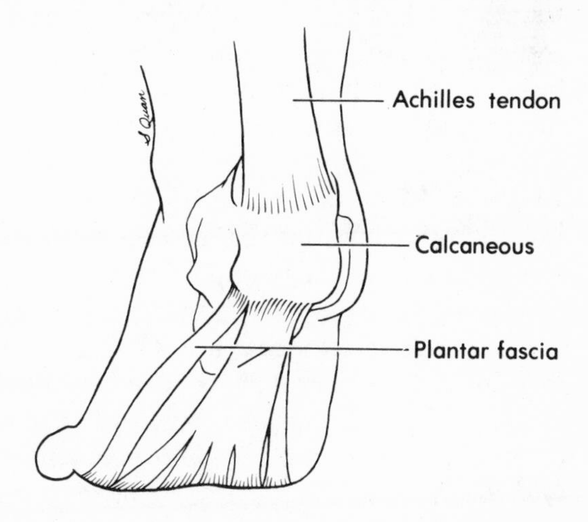

The problems of the foot could be the subject of an entire book, but here we'll consider only prevalent soft-tissue rheumatic foot problems. One condition, known commonly as a *heel spur* and medically as *plantar fasciitis,* causes pain in the heel on the bottom of the foot. The symptoms are pain in the heel with walking or standing and the sensation of having a pebble in the shoe. This is usually due to repeated minor injuries to the fascia where it attaches to the heel bone, or calcaneus. Such activities as frequent walking on concrete, or jogging or running, may bring it on. The inflammation is relatively deep and lies under some rather thick tissues of the foot. The treatment of this condition differs somewhat from that for other forms of tendinitis, the main trick being to take the pressure off the heel and let the inflammation subside. Your shoemaker may be of great assistance in supplying some soft heel pads with holes in the center. You can devise something like this yourself from a firm type of foam rubber. Your pharmacist will be able to supply some commercial materials that you can use for this purpose. Also, a shoe with a soft and thick sole may be of value.

Other areas of the plantar fascia, such as the arch of the foot, are subject to similar types of inflammation. Tendons in the foot can also become inflamed, a condition that can be confused with an acute attack of gout, particularly when the painful area is at the base of the big toe.

The Chest

Before discussing some of the rheumatic chest pains, I want to make one extremely important point:

Although some chest pains are due to musculoskeletal problems, some very serious ones are not. If you have chest pains, do not delay in seeing your physician. The major concern, of course, is that the chest pain could be due to underlying heart disease.

Chest pains can be due to a narrowing of the coronary arteries. The symptoms of coronary artery disease are extremely varied, and I have seen some tragic cases where people have considered these feelings of pressure or pain as just "strain," "indigestion," or "a tightness in the throat" when the discomfort has actually been a prelude to a heart attack. Other structures and organs in the chest, such as the esophagus, aorta, and lungs, may also be a source of pain.

Chest wall pains, however, can have a most benign origin: the tissues of the chest wall itself or, as referred pain, soft tissues elsewhere. One of the more common benign conditions that may be confused with heart pain is strain or inflammation of the cartilages that join the ribs to the sternum. The pain can be in any of the cartilage areas but is usually found at the left border of the sternum at the junction of the middle and lower thirds. The term given to this condition is *costochondritis,* which simply means inflammation of the rib cartilages. It often follows exercise or an injury sustained by such motions as heavy lifting. The pain may be present at rest or only with certain body motions. A physician diagnoses the condition by simply pressing these tender areas with the fingers or reproducing the pain with certain arm or shoulder motions.

One of the more widespread but less well-known types of chest pain and discomfort is that which begins in a very localized area of the spine between the shoulder blades. Considering the number of people who have it, it's surprising that someone hasn't given it a specific name. For our purposes, let's call it *spinous tendinitis*. The symptoms can range from a dull ache to an intermittent or persistent pain radiating around to the front of the chest. This condition can be due to an acute strain or, at times, to chronic poor posture. It is common in desk workers and can be extremely fatiguing or almost disabling. It responds well to postural exercises in most cases but can be a lingering nuisance.

A Real Pain in the Posterior

How often have you heard the statement that something is a "pain in the . . . posterior"? As in the case of Achilles' tendinitis, I am almost certain that the phrase "pain in the rear" owes its origin to people who have truly suffered with this discomfort. There are innumerable causes of pain in the buttock, vaginal, and rectal areas. A discussion of the various diagnoses, which might include one or more ruptured lumbar discs, infections, muscle tension, and even tumors, is beyond the scope of this book. Some of these causes, however, may be benign (but painful) conditions that fall under the heading of tendinitis.

A typical case is that of a forty-eight-year-old seamstress who limped into my office with a previous diagnosis of sciatica from a ruptured lumbar disc in her lower back. She couldn't sit on the left buttock because of pain. She had pain radiating down the back of her left leg and was fatigued because of lack of sleep. The basis of her problem turned out to be a condition known as *ischial bursitis*, a form of tendinitis commonly known as *weaver's bottom*. The *ischia* are bones that are part of the pelvis. When you sit, you sit on parts of your ischia. If the tendon and muscle attachments to the ischia are inflamed, you will be a little more comfortable standing or lying than sitting.

Multiple Areas of Tendinitis

Up to this point we've concentrated on specific areas of tendinitis. It isn't unusual, however, to find many parts of an individual's musculoskeletal system affected by tendinitis simultaneously. When many areas suddenly become inflamed, it's no surprise that patient and doctor alike think of a generalized arthritic problem as the cause of the discomfort. Why many tendons and related tissues can be involved at the same time is a matter for speculation. I feel fairly certain that hereditary factors play a strong role in this, since there is often a family history of these problems. I recall a very healthy and athletic Swiss woman in her early twenties who had tendinitis in her shoulders, hips, and elbows. Her twin sister had the identical problem. Both women had completely normal blood studies, but tiny clumps of calcium deposits were visible on X-ray examinations of their areas of pain.

Many people are diagnosed as having rheumatoid arthritis because they have pain near many joints, despite the facts that they have completely normal blood studies and X-ray examinations, and no swollen joints at all. I recall the story of one thirty-six-year-old businessman who carried the diagnosis of rheumatoid arthritis for sixteen years—once diagnosed, erroneously, he never sought another opinion. Finally, after being assured by a rheumatologist that he had a mild generalized form of tendinitis and after receiving a few days' treatment of anti-inflammatory agents, he was 95 percent better and has remained so. I suspect that much of his pain relief came from simply knowing the benign nature of his problem rather than from the effects of the medication.

By the way, it is certainly possible to have *both* arthritis and tendinitis. Distinguishing between these disorders is extremely important for proper and effective treatment.

VENEREAL DISEASE AND TENDINITIS

There are many ways of getting tendinitis, and surprisingly enough, sexual contact is one of them. This type of tendinitis is due not to stress or trauma to the tendons but to an infection by the bacteria that cause *gonorrhea.* The incidence of this problem is rising in this country, and knowledge of the association between these two conditions needs to be more widespread.

We used to think that anyone, male or female, who had gonorrhea showed symptoms soon after becoming infected. Now we know differently. The infection can be totally without symptoms in a man or woman for many months. This is one of the reasons that gonorrhea spreads so easily and is so difficult to eradicate in the population. Many people carry the infection without knowing it.

The "bug" that causes gonorrhea is called the *gonococcus*. It can get into the bloodstream and be disseminated throughout the body. In women, this usually occurs after a menstrual period. The gonococcus can cause a rash, fever, arthritis, meningitis, peritonitis, and various other problems. One common symptom associated with nonsexual areas of the body is a tendinitis accompanied by a fever.

The tendinitis caused by gonococcus bacteria can "migrate"; that is, it can move—and often does—from one tendon to another before settling in one or more joints. This is quite different from the types of tendinitis we've been discussing and is certainly more serious.

Gonococcus is not the only bacteria that can cause tendinitis, so if you have an infectious tendinitis, it by no means indicates that you have gonorrhea. The important point to remember is that tendinitis with fever suggests infection. If you have this combination of symptoms, get to a doctor.

SPRAINS, STRAINS, AND MUSCLE SPASMS

Sprains and strains are due to injury and differ from the inflammations that have been discussed so far. A sprain is a joint injury in which a partial tear of one or more ligaments occurs. If a sprain is severe, you may need to consult an orthopedic surgeon. A strain, often referred to as a "pull," is an injury to a muscle, tendon, or fascia that occurs by overstretching or overexerting. Mild strains respond to rest, analgesics, and physical therapy; more severe ones may require a doctor's attention.

Muscle spasms are involuntary contractions of a muscle or group of muscles, and the result is pain and limited function. There are many causes of muscle spasms, including a decreased blood supply, injury, infection, neurological diseases, and metabolic disturbances. The treatment depends on the cause.

CONCEPTS OF TREATMENT

Many treatments are available for the disorders in the tendinitis group. The variety of therapies is accounted for by the fact that no single form of treatment rids 100 percent of sufferers of the disorder. If one "cure" existed, all others would be superfluous. You may read articles and books that promise a cure by "my method," but I can only caution you against being too gullible, since disappointment may well follow. Experience has shown, however, that practically every sufferer with tendinitis can get relief from one or another treatment or from a combination of therapies.

Let's turn now to an overview of methods for preventing and treating tendinitis. Since many of these techniques and therapies are effective for other forms of soft-tissue rheumatism, the descriptions here will be brief, with more detailed information later on.

The Prevention of Tendinitis

Methods of preventing tendinitis are based on what we know of the causes of tendinitis. As you may recall, two major causes are poor conditioning and excessive straining of muscles and tendons.

If you plan to do any activity that will put a lot of stress on your muscles or tendons, or that requires frequent repetitive motions, you have at least two options. You can perform the activity in short periods, resting in between, or take a lesson from the athletes and gradually condition yourself for what you plan to do. Pace yourself. Work into the activity gradually. Don't try to become a long-distance runner or tennis pro overnight.

Over the past few thousand years, the human mind has devised myriad tools and implements not only for work but also for fun. We have ample opportunity to use many of these devices improperly, excessively, or both. The result can well be a roaring case of tendinitis. It follows, then, that we should choose the tools we use for work and sport to fit ourselves as individuals, a far simpler task than molding the individual to fit the device. It also follows that we have to consider the ability of our tissues, as well as the devices we have chosen, to withstand stress. All this sounds pretty obvious in theory, but it's a different story in practice. Consider a few examples.

I have seen (and ridden on) bicycle seats that are almost guaranteed to give you ischial bursitis. Tennis rackets and bats heavy enough for Goliath are still being sold to David. Screws and bolts are still being put in place and removed with tools that even Atlas couldn't get a good grip on. The lesson here is to choose your tools properly. Your best guide is common sense. Anticipate the job, think out your approach, and if you begin to feel undue stress on your muscles and tendons, back off. Even if you use the proper tools, remember that soft tissues will often give way before wood, iron, or steel.

Sometimes, though, despite our best efforts to use our muscles and tendons wisely, tendinitis occurs anyway. In such instances we need to turn our attention to methods of treatment.

Rest and Exercise—A Balance

Many people ask, "What's best for my tendinitis—rest or exercise?"

Either rest or exercise may help, or it may make little difference. If either were the cure, life would be simpler. The fact is, both have their place in the prevention and treatment of tendinitis.

When tissues are acutely inflamed and painful, resting the area often gives much relief. In some cases, rest alone may suffice to bring the discomfort under control. There is a limit to the benefit of rest, however. If it is prolonged over many weeks or months, certain adverse effects occur. The muscles become weaker, blood tends to pool in the extremity, and various deleterious reactions take place in the autonomic nerves that supply the area. Rest, therefore, is helpful to a point and inappropriate beyond that point. The question is, where is the point? There are individual differences, but the answer is that probably one or two weeks will tell you whether or not you're getting anywhere. If you're not, more than rest is needed for therapy.

Now let's consider the effects of exercise. If an area is inflamed, more activity of the muscles and tendons will increase the pain and inflammation. During the height of inflammation, therefore, exercise is the wrong approach. When the pain and discomfort begin to subside, that is the time to cautiously begin exercising. If things get worse, you have to back off. If they get better, you can increase the exercise.

There is a balance, then, between the beneficial effects of rest and exercise. Each has its place.

Heat or Cold?

Pain relief comes in many forms, and certainly the application of heat is one of the oldest remedies around and one that most people are familiar with. A lesser-known fact is that cold applications are also of value in the treatment of tendinitis. Again, each has its place, but what is the place for each?

The answer lies in whether or not the inflammation is *acute* or *chronic*. When an inflammation appears acutely (suddenly) and with pain, the application of cold packs tends to give more relief than heat. This is because the inflammatory process itself, with its various degrees of heat, redness, swelling, and pain, slows down in cold environments and increases in warm environments. Acute bursitis of the shoulder, for example, often responds best to cold. When inflammatory processes have been present for a long time—that is, when they are chronic—the body attempts to repair the damage by increasing the blood flow to the area. This process is helped by warmth. These are not hard-and-fast rules but are based on practical experience.

Liniments

Liniments applied locally over the area of pain are often useful for temporary relief. They have no effect on the underlying inflammation. The mechanism of pain relief is that of a *counterirritant*. The active ingredient in most liniments, methyl salicylate, mildly irritates the skin and appears to stimulate nerve endings that lead to the suppression of pain perception.

Splints and Other Supports

The temporary splinting of an area involved with tendinitis or related conditions may be necessary to help avoid motion and pain. Elastic bands worn around inflamed areas of the elbow, wrist, and knee give some people small relief of discomfort, but they give no real support. It's important, however, that they be kept loose enough to permit unrestricted blood flow to the rest of the extremity.

Physical Therapy

Many effective forms of treatment for the tendinitis group fall under the heading of physical therapy and can be administered by licensed physical therapists. Physical therapy techniques can include the application of heat or cold by many means and the use of various exercises to restore joint motion and muscle strength. It is surprising how rapidly muscle weakness can appear when a limb is put to rest. Rehabilitation should begin as soon as possible to prevent weakness and further susceptibility to muscle strain and inflammation.

Medications

Aspirin is the most widely used nonprescription drug for treating pain and inflammation. This mild analgesic (painkiller) has moderate but definite anti-inflammatory effects. Another drug with analgesic properties, acetaminophen, is also available without a prescription and is found in many drug combinations under many trade names. Acetaminophen, unlike aspirin, has *no* anti-inflammatory properties and is therefore less effective for the treatment of disorders in the tendinitis group.

At times discomfort can be so great that pain relief is the sufferer's primary concern. Codeine, a narcotic, and related drugs can be very helpful for the relief of pain, but narcotic drugs are potentially addictive and should be used sparingly and as briefly as possible. They are legally obtained only through a doctor's prescription.

Muscle relaxants, which are also prescription drugs, can help relieve pain by relieving muscle spasm. They are not inherently analgesics and have no effect on inflammation.

A newer group of medications has become available and has gained wide acceptance by patients and doctors alike. This group is known by the rather long title of nonsteroidal anti-inflammatory drugs, or *NSAIDs.* The term *nonsteroidal* means that they are not related to cortisone, which is a steroid. They have both analgesic and anti-inflammatory effects and often appear to be superior to aspirin. These drugs may have undesirable side effects, as does aspirin. They are available by prescription, and the group includes such drugs as indomethacin, ibuprofen, naproxen, and sulindac. Many other NSAIDs are on the market, and undoubtedly there are many more to come.

One of the most effective, and certainly the most rapid, forms of pain relief is the injection of medications directly into the site of inflammation by a physician trained in the technique. Sufferers often experience pain relief in minutes from the injection of a local anesthetic such as lidocaine. Injections of small amounts of a cortisone derivative such as prednisolone into the site of inflammation have long-lasting anti-inflammatory effects. The amount of prednisolone used is too small to have any detectable effect on the body itself, and injecting it puts it directly where it is needed. Many physicians use a mixture of both lidocaine and prednisolone to obtain rapid pain relief and long-lasting anti-inflammatory effects.

4

Those Puzzling Pains: Fibrositis

WHAT IT IS

Everybody has aches and pains. Suppose you exercised muscles that you used infrequently or you caught the flu or you got unusually chilled one day—you probably wouldn't be surprised to wake up stiff and sore the next morning. But suppose these symptoms occurred with no obvious explanation, and suppose they didn't go away. Say they just appeared, seemingly from nowhere, and lingered on and on, tiring you out and making you start to wonder just what was going on in your body. You'd probably go from disregard, to irritation, to downright worry and concern.

Finally you'd go to your doctor, who would run some tests, find them all to be negative, and urge you to take it easy—lighten up your work load, go on a vacation. But, to complete this classic scenario, say you just weren't able to convince yourself that everything was okay. Lingering pain means something's awry—everybody knows that. Just what, you'd ask yourself for the millionth time, is really the matter with me? A very likely answer in the case described would be *fibrositis*.

Fibrositis is the stepchild of the rheumatic diseases. For years some authorities denied its existence altogether; fortunately, these days such nonbelievers constitute a dwindling minority. At best, fibrositis has been neglected and misunderstood, and until recently it was basically overlooked in the medical profession's drive to conquer rheumatism and, of course, arthritis. But the enigmatic and age-old disorder we now call fibrositis is finally beginning to yield some of its secrets.

Fibrositis is unique among the soft-tissue rheumatic diseases because its causes often lie in that delicate balance between body and mind—or soma and psyche. As a result, fibrositis generally produces discomfort of a far greater intensity than laboratory reports alone would suggest. The explanation is that lab reports show only the physical side of things—the soma in the soma-psyche pairing. To understand fibrositis, one must focus on this complex and subtle bond. If you have fibrositis, the success of your treatment will depend greatly on a full understanding of the condition. Let's begin our journey toward this goal with some stories drawn from real life.

CASE HISTORIES

Betsy was thirty-eight years old. She had been divorced for three years when her symptoms appeared, and her financial situation was degenerating rapidly. With three children and a home to maintain, she had studied hard to earn her real estate license and had gone to work two years before for the first time in her life. Attractive, personable, and competent, for a while Betsy seemed to be pulling it all off—working full time, caring for her children, and assiduously tending her home. Sure she had worries—who didn't? But she kept them to herself. Above all, she was determined to make it on her own, *never* to be dependent on another person again.

Just when Betsy began to feel less like a beginner at work and more like a competent real estate agent, something happened that increasingly distracted her from her myriad responsibilities: She began to "hurt all over." Mild pains that she'd been feeling in her shoulders for some time—and successfully ignoring—now failed to recede as they once had.

Instead, they began to spread to her upper back and neck. Every morning when she woke up, she felt stiff. "But that's natural," she told herself, "because I sleep so hard." Now, however, the stiffness was staying with her all day, every day, impeding her every move and tiring her out too early. Simultaneously, her sleep became very restless, and she began to have headaches. The combination of symptoms was taking a tremendous toll on her energy. Morning and evening, Betsy was exhausted. "I just can't do it," she'd moan as she thought about shopping and making dinner after work, bathing and putting the kids to bed after dinner, and finishing the laundry and the vacuuming she'd begun before they woke up.

During the first few weeks when her symptoms surfaced and failed to go away, Betsy thought she had the flu. But gradually thoughts of more serious diseases entered her mind. Could it be that something dangerous was happening to her, she wondered? What would happen to her children if she couldn't work? What would happen to her? It wasn't long before Betsy's fantasies ran away with her and she'd worked herself into a panic.

After a month of increasing discomfort, Betsy decided to see her doctor. Her laboratory tests were all normal, and her doctor assured her that she was in good health. He prescribed rest and aspirin, and told her to call back if she was no better in a few weeks. The news relieved Betsy's mind a little, but it didn't reduce the pain. She experienced no improvement at all in the weeks that followed but felt reluctant to go back to her doctor. Instead, she decided to try some health store remedies on her own—natural foods, careful diet, and vitamin supplements. Nothing she did had any effect whatever on her symptoms. She became convinced that she had arthritis and decided to see a rheumatologist.

Betsy didn't have arthritis or any of the crippling or fatal diseases she had worried about. She had fibrositis. Her relief at the news was nearly palpable. She was eager to learn why she had been feeling so miserable and was ready to do anything she could to improve her condition. Armed with a new understanding of what was happening to her and with a simple but comprehensive treatment program, she was soon comfortable, confident, and fully engaged in her busy life.

Bill, a thirty-two-year-old shipping executive, had recently moved from New York City to the San Francisco area. He had long felt pain and discomfort in his shoulders and upper and lower back, and was now experiencing new discomfort in his hips, elbows, and knees. And he felt stiff and achy all day long. In giving his medical history to a rheumatologist, he spoke of a football injury to his right knee that he had sustained in high school, about fifteen years earlier. A month after he received the injury, the pain and swelling had basically disappeared, but when Bill was twenty-four it returned and continued to recur intermittently for the next eight years. A doctor told him that he might have a torn cartilage in his knee, and a blood test showed a slightly positive rheumatoid factor, a specific protein found in the blood of most people who have rheumatoid arthritis. Therefore, the doctor suggested, rheumatoid arthritis was also a possible diagnosis.

The rheumatologist asked Bill to talk a bit about his life. Bill said he was under a lot of stress at work. He spent most of his time on the phone juggling ship sailing schedules and cargoes to the Far East. Some days he barely had time to eat lunch. The vague pains and stiffness he had been feeling in his shoulders and his upper and lower back hadn't made things any easier, and his continually swelling knee impeded his mobility. As he talked, he referred more than once to the possibility, raised by his former doctor, that he might have rheumatoid arthritis, and he seemed convinced that this was indeed the explanation. Fear invaded his voice as he asked questions about the disease and about how much crippling he could expect.

The truth was that Bill had two separate problems. The

first was indeed a torn cartilage in the knee stemming from his old football injury. The second was fibrositis. Bill had latched onto the casual suggestion made on the basis of a blood test a long time ago, unaware that at least 5 percent of the normal, healthy population have a positive rheumatoid factor in the blood and that the test by no means verifies a diagnosis of rheumatoid arthritis. Once his separate problems were distinguished and diagnosed, Bill could be treated—and his treatment was very successful.

Janet is a fifty-two-year-old bookkeeper. She's attractive, physically active, and deeply involved in her happy home and social life. For about eighteen months before attending to it, she had been experiencing a "catch" in her right hip. Soon more symptoms showed up: aching in her upper and lower back and buttocks, and pains radiating down her right leg. The more she rested, the worse the pains became. Her arms and legs began to tingle, and she felt as though her hands and feet were swelling. The symptoms began to overwhelm her; soon she gave up doing housework and turned the chores over to her husband and two children. She became careless and indifferent to her work, and she put on a lot of weight. Every day Janet felt more and more disabled. She cried a lot, slept poorly, and was miserable all the time.

The first doctor Janet consulted was an orthopedic surgeon. He suspected a ruptured lumbar disc and sciatica (pain down the back of the leg caused by pressure on the sciatic nerve). But despite two more opinions—from a neurosurgeon and a neurologist—and a series of very expensive and sophisticated tests, the diagnosis of a lumbar disc problem was never confirmed. Throughout this mystery story, while doctors searched for the leading clue, Janet was treated with a potpourri of anti-inflammatory medicines, painkillers, and injections. Though Janet became hopeful with every new prescription, nothing helped for very long.

What was going on? Where were all these pains coming

from? You might suspect by now that I haven't told you the full story and you'd be right. To begin with, Janet's life wasn't at all the peaches and cream she wanted people to believe it was, although you'd probably be fooled if you spoke with her yourself. For starters, her sister, who lived across the street, hadn't spoken to her for six years. In fact, many of Janet's relatives lived in the area, and half of them didn't speak to the other half. Janet was a sensitive and loving person, and she felt terrible about the feuds and bad feelings rampant in her family. But being "strong" and immune to petty squabbles, she said, she refused to let herself show her angry and hurt feelings. Her husband showed no interest in her family at all, so Janet was on her own, left to cope with the situation in any way she could. Janet felt depressed fairly often but attributed her negative feelings to "those darn pains in my leg and back." "Those darn pains," by the way, had effectively wiped out her sex life. By the time she sought help again, she was still putting on a brave face but she felt isolated and depressed all the time.

It's no wonder that Janet's symptoms failed to respond to what seemed like adequate medical therapy. The initial spark that had ignited her pain and discomfort was trochanteric bursitis. However, the fuel that kept her misery going was not inflammation but a reaction involving mind and body: a round robin of tension, anxiety, and stress resulting in depression and physical pain. This cycle was as far from being under her conscious control as a migraine headache would have been. Janet had no wish to be ill, but because she had no understanding of her condition, she had no means of breaking the cycle of tension and pain.

It will come as no surprise to learn that Janet had a full-blown case of fibrositis. She didn't begin to improve until she was able to come to grips with her major problem: her inability to express her feelings about what she considered to be foolish family quarrels that were never resolved. At the height of her discomfort, she turned her anger inward, where it manifested itself as muscle tension. Through education and retraining, she was able to express, rather than suppress, her feelings, thus greatly relieving her symptoms. This new way of behaving, coupled with an active physical therapy program, markedly increased Janet's sense of well-being—and dramatically improved her sex life.

The hallmarks of fibrositis, as these three stories suggest, are diffuse aches plus pain and stiffness anywhere in the back or neck and around almost any joint. Still, as the case histories again make clear, fibrositis manifests itself differently in different individuals, a fact that might account for the difficulty of diagnosing it accurately. Sufferers variously describe their pain as deep, burning, knifelike, sharp, dull, needlelike, steady, intermittent, fatiguing, gnawing, spasmodic, throbbing, and cramping—the list goes on and on. As we have seen, pain, like taste and smell, can be perceived in many different ways.

Most people with fibrositis experience their aches and pains most intensely in the morning and at night, although this too varies among sufferers. And the pains may ebb and flow or remain steadily present—often for many years. Generally, stiffness accompanies the aches and pains, and it is frequently—though temporarily—alleviated by exercise.

Other frequently reported symptoms are feelings of fatigue or exhaustion, even after the patient has had a good rest. Normal sleep patterns may be disrupted with tossing and turning. Very often, patients whose joints appear perfectly normal insist that their joints feel swollen, which adds to the total discomfort. Intermittent feelings of numbness and tingling are also frequently reported, as are headaches and an inability to tolerate cold. And fibrositis is commonly accompanied by diarrhea or constipation, often in the alternating pattern known as irritable bowel syndrome.

As stressed earlier, emotional upsets as well as physical discomforts are almost always a part of the fibrositis disorder. Anxiety, tension, suppressed anger, and depression are found with great frequency. Usually, both doctors and patients attribute these feelings to the presence of the physical symptoms: Who wouldn't feel anxious, tense, angry, or depressed at having to live with pain and stiffness all the time? Most often, however, the emotional symptoms are related to the *cause* rather than the effects of fibrositis itself. That is, the high anxiety and depression *precede* and are made worse by the fibrositis. One can neither understand nor treat the physical symptoms of fibrositis without appreciating the importance of this fact.

To summarize, the main symptoms of fibrositis are persistent aches, pains, and stiffness. Other associated symptoms include fatigue, exhaustion, numbness, feelings of swelling in the joints, irritable bowel syndrome, anxiety, cold intolerance, disturbed sleep, tingling, headaches, tension, suppressed anger, and depression. Fibrositis is truly a disorder with many faces.

WHO GETS IT?

Fibrositis is not a rare disorder; in fact, it is a very common one. Still, for several reasons, coming up with exact figures on the incidence of fibrositis is difficult. One reason is that many people have a mild form of the disease and never see a doctor about it. Another is that fibrositis is often diagnosed as something else and is therefore recorded as arthritis or some other problem. Still another reason is that fibrositis is what you might call an a.k.a., or "also known as," disease. Over the years, fibrositis has been given many different names in the medical literature, and recognizing the disease behind this jumble of terms can take some real detective work. Despite the confusion, however, we now know a substantial amount about the disease and have some fairly reliable, if general, statistics on the types of people most likely to suffer from it.

Since 1981, the American journal *Arthritis and Rheu-*

matism has published three studies categorizing the diagnoses of patients seen in rheumatology offices. In one of the two studies done in the United States, 5 percent of all patients seen were diagnosed as having fibrositis;[1] in the other the figure was 16 percent.[2] The third study, done in Mexico City, showed that 15 percent of the patients seen had fibrositis.[3] Further, a report from the Peoria School of Medicine based on a study of 285 new patients seen in a rheumatology clinic in 1979 showed that fibrositis accounted for 20 percent of the diagnoses.[4] This figure was exceeded only by osteoarthritis, diagnosed in 29 percent of the cases. The report showed too that fibrositis was the most common diagnosis (33 percent) in patients under fifty years of age. These figures tend to confirm the notion that fibrositis is a major medical problem afflicting millions of people.

We also know that women are much more prone to fibrositis than men, though we don't know why this is so. In fact, out of every eight sufferers, seven are women. The disease tends to strike women either around their mid-thirties or at the time of menopause, a fact that shatters the myth that rheumatism of any type is a condition of old age. Actually, almost no age group is immune to fibrositis: One of the youngest patients reported in the medical literature was only five years old.

The expansion of our knowledge of human genetics has made us all more aware of our hereditary backgrounds. In this regard I have frequently been asked whether there is a genetic basis to fibrositis or, to put it another way, whether the disease "runs in families." To date, no evidence has been discovered to suggest that one can inherit a definite susceptibility to fibrositis, though the possibility still exists. In my own experience the disease does appear to strike mothers and their daughters more frequently than would be expected were its occurrence completely random. However, such a mother-daughter link, if indeed it exists, might be explained as well by environmental as by genetic factors. Thus, we will have to gain more knowledge about fibrositis before we can answer questions concerning inherited tendencies and other genetic relationships.

Another frequently asked question is whether a particular personality type contributes to the risk of getting the disease. The answer to this one is an unqualified yes. Fibrositis is most frequently seen in those who have one or more of the following characteristics: perfectionism, compulsiveness, tension, anxiety, feelings of suppressed hostility or frustration, and depression. Fibrositis patients are frequently very intelligent, hard-driving, aggressive, and productive people who put a high value on achievement and success.

Clearly, knowing the characteristics of those most likely to get the disease is a great aid in diagnosis. Let's look now at that delicate art, the cornerstone of the physician's practice.

DIAGNOSING FIBROSITIS

When I was in medical school, one of my professors facetiously identified the three most important aspects of making a diagnosis as the history, the history, and the history. His point was that in most disorders the best clues to a medical problem are found not in the results of lab reports and X rays but in what the patient tells the doctor—in response to the right questions, of course. This approach is certainly the best where fibrositis is concerned.

If you think you might have fibrositis, you can begin to check out your suspicion by asking yourself a few pertinent questions: Do you consider yourself tense? Are there unresolved stresses in your job, your marriage, your social life? Do you often feel like crying? Are you frequently depressed? Be warned that in this introspective process you are sure to come up against certain psychological defenses, since you'll need to ascertain what your true feelings are on some fundamental issues in your personal history. For some of us it's easy to talk honestly about our deep feelings; for others it's nearly impossible. But both the diagnosis and treatment of fibrositis depend on one's effort to break through defenses that block deep feeling. Remember, fibrositis is a result of the interaction of body and mind—soma and psyche. History, history, history—which covers emotional and psychological experiences as well as physical ones—is the key to determining the truth.

Besides the psychological clues gathered through honest self-examination, certain physical evidence will point to the possibility of fibrositis and in fact must be present to confirm the diagnosis. This evidence consists of the presence of "tender points" over various muscle groups, especially those in the area of the neck, shoulders, hips, and back. Pressing these areas causes pain and discomfort far above that normally expected.

In some of the literature you may also read of "trigger points"—places on the body that, when pressed, trigger pains in other places. Fibrositis sufferers can have tender points, trigger points, or both. Another characteristic of fibrositis often described in the literature is the presence of palpable firm nodules in the tender areas of the muscles. About a hundred years ago the German medical literature contained long articles about these nodules, and it was the prevailing opinion that where these nodules were not present the diagnosis was not fibrositis (though the Germans referred to the condition with a host of descriptive German terms, not *fibrositis*). These days, however, many physicians consider the presence of nodules unnecessary to the diagnosis.

Besides the tenderness noted above, no other physical evidence is involved in a diagnosis of fibrositis. For example, findings of joint swelling or a skin rash would suggest something else or something else plus fibrositis. Nor are physical factors that might be detected in a blood test or X ray related to fibrositis. Where abnormal studies are present, we're back to something else or to something else plus fibrositis. In pure fibrositis, all tests are normal. However, a physician trying to determine the presence of fibrositis is likely to order some studies to make certain the patient has no other problem. So if your doctor asks you to get blood tests or X rays, don't be worried or surprised.

Now comes a word of caution with a capital C. By now you realize that fibrositis isn't the easiest disorder to diagnose. Furthermore, some diseases mimic fibrositis closely enough to confound even the most astute diagnostician. These include polymyalgia rheumatica, temporal arteritis, and hypothyroidism (all discussed in later chapters). Such diseases can have some *extremely* serious consequences unless treated properly (the treatments are effective, I might add), so *don't make the final diagnosis* yourself. Get help from a doctor. Explain your symptoms and get a second opinion (your own perhaps being the first). Even if you're a doctor yourself, you'll need some assistance in confirming the diagnosis. Another bit of wisdom I picked up in medical school was that those who serve as their own doctors have fools for doctors and fools for patients. A biting comment, perhaps, but true where many disorders are concerned, fibrositis among them.

Before leaving the diagnosis of fibrositis it may be useful to list some of the myriad terms given to fibrositis in the past. You may well have read articles about this disorder without knowing it. The name fibrositis was introduced by W. R. Gowers in 1904.[5] Some of the "also known as" terms follow:

Fat herniations
Fibromyalgia
Fibromyositis
Interstitial myofibrositis
Muscular rheumatism
Myalgia
Myofascial pain syndrome
Myofasciitis
Myofibrositis
Neurofibrositis
Pain amplification syndrome
Scapulocostal syndrome
Tension myalgia
Tension rheumatism
Traumatic myofibrositis

WHAT CAUSES IT?

If you have fibrositis, understanding the causes of your disease will be central to the success of your treatment. In this section, therefore, I take care to trace the origins of fibrositis in a detailed way. You'll notice that I say origins—plural, not singular. A cluster of factors causes fibrositis, a fact that makes understanding just that much more difficult and that much more important.

Let's begin by eliminating what are *not* the causes of fibrositis. The disease is not an infectious one; there are no bacteria, viruses, fungi, or parasites involved. Therefore, it is impossible to catch it or give it to anyone. Also, there is no evidence that diet plays any significant role in fibrositis. The disorder can apparently occur regardless of what the sufferer eats—vegetarian, "natural foods," junk food, and fish are all without effect. Regarding the new environmental pollutants with which we are increasingly surrounded, it's unlikely that they play much of a role in fibrositis, since the symptoms of the disease have been around for well over a hundred years and there is also no evidence to suggest that the incidence of fibrositis is higher in polluted than nonpolluted areas.

Finally, hormonal imbalances have been well studied and are apparently without effect where fibrositis is concerned. I am frequently asked by patients about one of these conditions in particular—namely, hypoglycemia. This condition is an abnormally low level of sugar in the blood, and in recent years it has been widely touted as the source of just about every discomfort one can name. Nearly all the physicians I have queried agree with me that hypoglycemia has no relation whatever to the symptoms of fibrositis. I have yet to see a patient with fibrositis whose symptoms are related to blood sugar level in any way.

That said, we can turn to the factors we know *are* involved in causing fibrositis. As suggested earlier, the strongest evidence points to a combination of factors originating in the body and mind. This body-mind pair is affected by environmental stimuli and stress. Let's start with a simple diagram showing the relationships among body, psychological stimuli, and stress (mediated by the mind) and environmental (or external) stimuli and stresses.

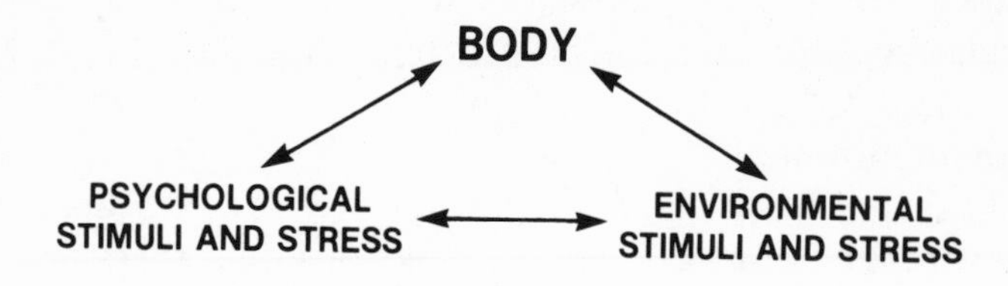

The body's organs and tissues generally respond to stimuli and stress in "normal," healthy ways. For example, if we are frightened, our bodies produce adrenaline, which constricts blood vessels in the intestines and dilates them in muscles. By improving blood flow to the muscles, this prepares us for the so-called fight or flight response. In sunlight, our pupils constrict to help prevent light from damaging our retinas. If we are hungry, even the smell of food will cause gastric acid and enzymes to enter our stomachs in preparation for digesting food. These are all examples of healthy responses to external stimuli.

Sometimes, however, our organs and tissues respond to stress or stimuli in ways that are detrimental to our health. For example, a tense situation may cause our blood pressure to rise to a dangerous level. Chronic tensions and concerns might lead to hyperacidity and duodenal ulcers. And other stimuli or stress can cause diarrhea or vomiting. Thus, for certain individuals, stress results in abnormal reactions. Where in the body those reactions occur will depend on the "target" organs of the particular person. These target organs vary among individuals, leading some people, for example, to develop stomach troubles when they are under stress while others suffer headaches. It is important to emphasize once more that many people respond to stress in healthy ways that have no ill effects whatever.

As may be obvious by now, the symptoms of fibrositis can be classified along with duodenal ulcers and high blood pressure as abnormal reactions to stress. For fibrositis sufferers, the target organs are primarily the muscles and their supporting tissues. Under conditions of chronic and often low-grade stimuli and stress, the muscles respond by remaining in a state of tension and, for reasons that are as yet unclear, by sending signals to the brain that are interpreted as pain, aching, and stiffness.

What types of low-grade stimuli and stress cause muscle tension under these circumstances, and how do the signals originate? For some, the stimuli might simply be poor posture while sitting and typing—or any other instance of poor muscle usage. However, sources of tension are in no way limited to poor body mechanics, as everybody knows. Just look around! Our world pummels us with stimuli and stresses morning, noon, and night. On a purely physical level, sights, sounds, and smells bombard our senses. In our social, work, and family lives most of us are constantly beset with demands, questions, ideas, and myriad obligations—to do, to be, to give, to take. "If it's not one thing, it's another," we say distractedly, longing for a time when we can just float along, simply *being*.

The stimuli and stresses originating outside our bodies can have another effect—and the mind side of the mind-body pair enters here. These stimuli can trigger psychological responses, determined by our personal conditioning and histories; these in turn can produce muscle tension in those susceptible to it. The psychological responses most likely to produce chronic muscle tensions include compulsiveness, anxiety, tension, suppressed anger, and depression.

To summarize, our bodies, minds, and the environment are constantly interacting. In people in whom this interaction causes chronic muscle tension, fibrositis is the result. Furthermore, the symptoms of the disease themselves cause psychological stress, which reduces that much more the sufferer's ability to deal effectively with the environment. In this way the environment-mind-body cycle completes itself, and fibrositis persists.

Though they may originate in psychological stress, the pain, stiffness, and aching of fibrositis are not imagined. These symptoms are as real as high blood pressure or duodenal ulcers, even though they cannot be seen or measured. The fact that these effects are invisible and unmeasurable has been a major impediment to the recognition and acceptance of fibrositis as a significant affliction. It also explains why fibrositis sufferers can undergo exhaustive batteries of studies only to be told that they are normal and well—despite their debilitating discomfort.

As unique individuals, we differ from one another in our reactions to stress and tension. Those of us whose bodies respond to stress with chronic muscular tension may have various secondary effects as well, again determined by our particular bodies and minds. Thus, the symptoms that accompany fibrositis in various individuals might be disturbed sleep, tingling, feelings of joint swelling, or any of the others described in the first section of this chapter.

RETRAIN: A RATIONAL APPROACH TO TREATMENT

The basic premise of any program for the treatment of fibrositis is this: The treatment must be tailored to the individual's specific needs. So many causative factors are involved in fibrositis, so many different forms of treatment exist, and so many individual responses to treatment are possible that a treatment program must be designed with careful attention to these multiple variables. Also—to reiterate an obvious point—the diagnosis of fibrositis must be correct for the carefully designed treatment to be effective. Again, certain disorders mimic fibrositis, and a physician's advice is necessary in determining whether or not fibrositis is present.

However, though the physician must initiate and oversee the treatment, the key to its success lies with the patient. As I have intimated before, without the patient's understanding and willingness to try, the treatment will probably fail.

Given the sufferer's wholehearted participation, the fundamental ingredient in a therapy program is *retraining*. Under medical guidance, fibrositis sufferers retrain their thinking, their muscles, and their responses to stress. What follows is a therapy program I call RETRAIN, which covers these basic areas:

R Rest and relaxation
E Education
T Therapeutic muscle training
R Responses to stress
A Analgesics
I Injections of muscle tender points
N Never give up hope!

R / Rest and Relaxation

Periods of rest and relaxation from daily stresses are necessary to break the mind-body-environment cycle causing fibrositis. The *R* in *RETRAIN* can also be translated as *Respite* or *Rehabilitation*. Even the United States Army recognizes the need for rest, and anyone who has served remembers fondly their two weeks of R and R!

By rest I do not mean the complete avoidance of exercise. In fact, if you have been active, complete rest may well make the fibrositis worse instead of better, since pent-up energy itself can become muscle tension and pain. The point is not simply to take to your bed but to do something you enjoy, something unrelated to anything that might create more tension. In this sense, *rest* might be walking in the woods, playing a game of checkers, or reading a good book. Your rest should be a diversion—something that separates you temporarily from what is causing you stress. However inactive your body might be, if your mind is not at ease, you are not really relaxing.

E / Education

As is surely clear by now, education is an essential component of a successful fibrositis therapy program. To eliminate the tension the disease itself might be causing, you must understand—and believe—that fibrositis is a benign disease, one that will not cripple, deform, or kill you, and that, despite your prior experience, the pain and stiffness you are suffering *can* be reversed.

T / Therapeutic Muscle Training

Like any material on earth, our muscles have their limitations, and they function best when they are used properly. When we let our muscles get weak, they perform poorly, and they respond to overuse with pain and stiffness. The same is true when we overstrain or abuse our muscles by practicing poor posture or by allowing emotional stress to become muscle tension. Still, even those who have abused their muscles all their lives can, through a program of therapeutic muscle and postural training, greatly reduce the resultant pain and stiffness and teach themselves to respond more normally to the unavoidable stresses of daily living. Such a program might include the application of heat or cold, massage, acupressure, hydrotherapy, or other forms of treatment that produce muscle relaxation.

R / Responses to Stress

Most would agree that it is impossible to avoid all environmental and emotional stresses. In fact, complete avoidance sounds like a rather poor idea. If it were possible, all progress would probably stop and life would become exceedingly dull.

Nevertheless, it stands to reason that if tensions and stresses can cause fibrositis, and if we can't always avoid those that are detrimental, the next best option would be to retrain our responses to them. That is, we might not be able to reduce the incoming stresses, but we can change our patterns of dealing with them to eliminate responses that are themselves problematic.

The goal, then, is to find better ways of responding to stress. As I noted earlier, stresses can be good or bad. When energy builds up within as a result of stress, the effects are negative—and something has to give. The solution is to let off some steam now and then. The mechanism you use for this will depend on what you are most comfortable with. If your muscle tension originates in suppressed anger that you really cannot express, perhaps a daily workout on a stationary bicycle would let out some of the built-up energy. Or if you're obsessively worried about deadlines at work and can't change your schedule, perhaps going to the movies would give your body and mind a vacation from your worries while you use up some trapped energy in thinking about the plot. You might well benefit simply from improving your posture by adjusting the height of your chair or worktable. But if the detrimental stresses result from a job, or from a marital or other social situation that cannot be easily changed or resolved, psychological or psychiatric counseling might be appropriate. There are all sorts of ways to do it—but you must choose *your* way.

A / Analgesics

Analgesics are agents that produce insensibility to pain. Simply put, an analgesic is a "painkiller." It's best to avoid analgesics as much as possible, since all these substances have undesirable side effects. Often, exercise, heat, and massage are effective as substitutes. However, there are times when analgesics are necessary as a temporary measure to help break the cycle that produces fibrositis. In these instances, the milder the medication the better. Aspirin or acetaminophen, which can be helpful, are available over the counter; stronger substances require a doctor's prescription. Muscle relaxants, though not true analgesics, can give relief, and other medications known as tricyclic antidepressants are effective in reducing pain perception. The NSAID (nonsteroidal anti-inflammatory drugs) group has effects similar to those of aspirin. The word *nonsteroidal* means that these substances are not related to steroids, and to cortisone in particular, an important fact to know. Cortisone and its derivatives are very effective medications in treating certain disorders, but they have limited usefulness with fibrositis. Some physicians inject small amounts into painful muscle areas, but the oral forms are generally ineffective in relieving symptoms and can have undesirable side effects such as weight gain, thinning of the bones, and easy bruising.

I / Injection of Muscle Tender Points

Many authorities recommend that muscle tender points be injected with varying combinations of lidocaine (a local anesthetic often used in dentistry too) and a cortisone preparation such as prednisolone or dexamethasone. Such injections might give temporary relief at times and constitute an acceptable form of therapy. If at all possible, however, it is preferable to avoid any form of injection and to rely instead on therapeutic muscle training.

Another medicinal approach is to spray on the skin a compound such as fluorimethane, which may help by setting up a neurological reflex that relaxes tense muscles. The fluorimethane evaporates very rapidly, causing localized cooling of the skin and a reflex relaxation of the underlying muscles. The effect is similar to that of putting an ice pack on the area. I have found this method to offer only temporary relief, but there are very strong advocates of its use and it is a very acceptable form of therapy.

N / Never Give Up Hope

Throughout the treatment, it is important to remember that fibrositis is a benign disease. It causes no crippling and no deformity. It is a treatable disorder, and its associated pain and stiffness can be relieved. Treating the disease will require some effort on your part, but you will be rewarded with a happier, more comfortable life. Whatever the course of your treatment once fibrositis has been confirmed, above all never give up hope!

5

Power of the Mind: The Psyche and Rheumatic Pains

SOMA AND PSYCHE REVISITED

As we have made clear, pain is both a universal and a subjective experience. Whenever it occurs, pain is a signal that something is wrong, that the one experiencing it is in some kind of danger. Despite the unpleasantness of painful feelings, our ability to perceive them protects us from harm. Thus we avoid touching hot stoves because we know from experience that to do so will bring pain and tissue damage in the form of burns. Even if we do inadvertently touch a hot stove, we experience pain and reflexively withdraw our hand even before appreciating the intellectual reasons for the action. If we move an arthritic joint or an inflamed muscle or tendon, pain warns us that further damage could occur if we persist.

Often, though, the pain we feel seems excessive—more than we need to warn us of danger. And it seems to outlive its usefulness as well. We feel it long after we burn ourselves, and we feel it in our inflamed muscles, tendons, and joints even at rest. In fact, in certain situations, pain—not the injury or disease it indicates—can become the overriding concern. In such instances the usefulness of pain and its beneficial nature as a warning against danger are lost. Instead, the pain itself is a major threat to our stability.

In an earlier chapter we touched on one other negative aspect of pain, the distress it gives by its nature—its appearance at times in the absence of any demonstrable physical injury or disease. That is, pain, supposedly the signal of a physical abnormality needing attention, appears on its own, unlinked to a detectable physical problem. This form of pain can cause as much suffering as pain that can be accounted for more straightforwardly, though detached observers are sometimes skeptical as to its intensity and even its reality. Pain of this sort can run the full gamut of intensity from mild to overwhelming, in the latter case becoming the very center of the sufferer's life. It can be a mere nuisance or a total disability; rather than being *caused by* a physical abnormality, great pain of this sort can actually *cause* physical problems.

In a sense, pain with no demonstrable cause can be a greater threat than the pain of injury or disease because the mystery of its source can frighten sufferers deeply. "Do I have a terminal disease?" they wonder. "Will I ever be normal again, or will my life be nothing but pain until I die?" Sometimes people with this kind of pain wind up devoting all their resources—physical, mental, and financial—to searching for nonexistent physical explanations for their misery. In this way, pain, though often our friend, can be a destructive enemy.

This chapter is devoted to the dark side of pain, as enemy and torturer. It focuses on what are called the psychogenic soft-tissue rheumatic complaints: *psycho* = mind; *genic* = origins. Here we will explore both pure psychogenic rheumatism—rheumatic disorders stemming purely from the psyche—and those situations in which psychogenic factors exaggerate existing rheumatic problems or secondarily cause muscular dysfunction and pain. In the course of the chapter it will be clear that feelings of pain can often be diminished by a deeper understanding of its origins. As Aristophanes said more than two thousand years ago, "The wise learn many things from their enemies."[1]

Case Histories

The patient was a deeply religious middle-aged man. In the course of his life he had been quite successful, not only financially but in his family and social life as well. He had ten children and was a philanthropic leader in his community. He had large land holdings and raised a variety of animals, primarily sheep. But through a series of misfortunes that were not of his making, he suffered severe financial losses. Other circumstances separated him from his children. To make matters worse, he developed a generalized skin infection. Despite the efforts of a few close friends, he became mentally depressed and experienced severe feelings of worthlessness. He was unable to sleep at night and constantly tossed and turned. He then developed severe rheumatic complaints—generalized and piercing musculoskeletal pains. Fortunately, a close friend, working on his behalf, was able to reverse not only the financial calamities but the family separations as well. The depression cleared, and as it did the patient's rheumatic complaints disappeared.

Sound familiar? The story is a brief synopsis of the biblical story of Job. Here's how Job himself describes his sleeplessness and body pains:

> And wearisome nights are appointed to me.
> When I lie down, I say, "When shall I arise?"
> But the night is long, and I am full of tossings
> to and fro until the dawning of the day.
>
> JOB 7:3–4

> Days of affliction have taken hold upon me.
> In the night my bones are pierced, and fall from me,
> And my sinews take no rest.
>
> JOB 30:16–17

In an eloquent article in the *Annals of Internal Medicine,* Morton A. Kapusta and Solomon Frank describe how chapter 30 in the Book of Job, written more than two thousand years ago, contains a modern, scientifically accurate description of mental depression associated with somatic symptoms. [2] Although we do not know for certain, the author or authors of the Book of Job may have recognized the association of soma and psyche.

Howard, a retired oil company executive, was sixty-seven years old. He had been seeing the same doctor for eighteen years, during which time he had annual physical examinations. Except for minor ailments, his health had always been good. But over the years his doctor noticed that Howard was slowly losing interest in his job, developing severe insomnia, and crying at times for no apparent reason. Howard also became verbally abusive to his family, to the point where his wife was threatening a divorce. It was apparent to his physician that Howard had developed a mental depression and that he was in need of psychiatric therapy. But Howard totally resisted any type of treatment, be it antidepressant medications or psychotherapy.

At age sixty-four he began complaining of pain in his neck, lower back, and shoulders. He sought medical opinions from eight other physicians, all of whom agreed that Howard was in a severe mental depression. Howard's answer was that anyone would be depressed with all the arthritic pain he was having, and he began showing suicidal tendencies. At age sixty-six he finally agreed to see a psychiatrist but still refused to take any kind of antidepressant medication. A year later Howard was still depressed, had lost a considerable amount of weight, and was constantly complaining of his "arthritic pains."

This man's mental depression was clearly diagnosed by his personal doctor and other physicians. His pain symptoms developed long after his depression began, but he insisted that the pain itself accounted for any depressed feelings he was having. His unfortunate decision to disregard the advice of the many competent physicians he saw deprived him of all hope of successful treatment.

Alicia had worked as a secretary for three months when she began having stiffness and aching in her legs and the upper part of her back. Her symptoms grew progressively worse, and she began to dread getting up in the morning. She had read that rheumatoid arthritis often strikes women in their twenties, and she was twenty-three years old. She consulted her physician, who did a thorough physical examination and ordered a variety of laboratory studies and X rays. She was tender over many muscle groups, but all the lab tests and X rays were normal. Her doctor suspected that she might be having early symptoms of rheumatoid arthritis and prescribed a regimen of aspirin and rest. She got no better, and the more she rested, the worse she felt. Alicia was certain that her joints were swelling, despite her doctor's reassurances to the contrary. In desperation she sought another opinion.

Supported by her husband, Alicia walked slowly into the new doctor's office. She told the doctor that she had been happily married for six months and that she wanted to work for a few years before raising a family. Prior to taking the secretarial job, she had been physically active and had taught courses in modern dance and exercise. But she was so anxious to be successful at her new job that she gave up all her physical activities to devote her time solely to her new profession. It was then that the pain and stiffness began. Her greatest fear, she said, was of the physical limitations she would suffer because of rheumatoid arthritis.

Alicia did not have rheumatoid arthritis; she had fibrositis, the soft-tissue rheumatic problem. The doctor's treatment consisted simply of an explanation of the problem and the advice that Alicia increase her physical activity and exercise. After two weeks on this regimen, her symptoms entirely disappeared.

Alicia's problem stemmed not from disease but from her suppression of her healthy abundance of energy. In dedicating herself to her sedentary job, she stopped releasing her excess energy through physical activities and thus it was directed into creating muscle tensions. Meanwhile, as she grew more tense, Alicia began to worry about the possibility that she had a debilitating disease. The more anxious she grew on this account, the tenser she grew physically, and her enforced rest only exaggerated this round robin of anxiety and muscle tension. In this situation, then, psychogenic factors—the worries and anxieties surrounding the imagined disease—made what might have been only a nuisance into a painful state and even a potential catastrophe.

Fred, thirty-seven years old, was the owner of a car-leasing business. He felt pain in back of both hip joints that had come on during a week-long hiking trip in the High Sierras. He had carried a heavy pack and felt certain that he had injured his hips or back. Fred's doctor, after appropriate studies, told him that his hip joints were normal and that the problem did not seem to be coming from his back. Fred was initially reassured, but as the pain persisted he convinced himself that he had gone to the doctor too early and that surely some type of arthritis would show up on his X ray now. He became tense and irritable with his family and left his office early on many occasions because of his pain. He then consulted another physician, who pinpointed the diagnosis—not arthritis but trochanteric bursitis. The doctor explained the possible treatments to him: first, a trial of anti-flammatory drugs and then, if they were ineffective, injections. He smiled and answered that "maybe the pain's not too bad after all; I think I can live with it."

The initial cause of Fred's problem was a bursitis. This condition can certainly be painful, but in this case Fred's perception of pain was heightened by the unknown and by his fear of serious disability. It is not at all unusual for patients who have taken strong painkillers to stop all medications and "learn to live with it" when they find their discomfort is neither life-threatening nor deforming. It often appears that a heavy weight has suddenly been lifted from them, and the intensity of the pain they feel rapidly diminishes.

Joanne was a twenty-year-old college student. She and her housemate spent a day refinishing some chairs and a table. The next day she noted pain in her right wrist near the base of the thumb. Her doctor diagnosed it as an inflammation of the tendon that runs to the thumb, prescribed an anti-inflammatory drug, and told her to avoid stressing the tendon.

Joanne was extremely concerned about the pain and the possibility of further injury, so she held her hand and arm rigidly at her side, not even moving her elbow. Within a few days the hand and wrist began to swell and the skin became warm and exquisitely tender. At times the skin would be cold and clammy. The more it hurt, the less Joanne moved it. She was unable to sleep and was in constant agony. After a week she returned to her doctor, who diagnosed her condition as reflex sympathetic dystrophy. The doctor made clear that it was absolutely essential for her to begin moving her arm, but she could not bear the pain and continued to hold it completely rigid. She required narcotics for the pain and also received sedation and an intensive course of physical therapy. The swelling and pain gradually subsided, and after four months her hand and wrist were normal again.

Reflex sympathetic dystrophy is a complex and poorly understood disease that apparently involves the autonomic nervous system (the system that controls the involuntary functions of the body). At times it is apparent that the psyche as well as somatic factors play a role in its causation. The disorder is inherently very painful, and the pain is often heightened to an intolerable degree by associated anxiety and fear.

Successful therapy is based on prompt medical intervention plus the reduction of anxieties and fears that inhibit the sufferer from moving the affected limb.

These case histories illustrate that psychogenic factors play a major role in the causation and perception of pain. Many shrug off the significance of "psychogenic pain," considering it to be "merely" imagined, hallucinated, or otherwise illusory. But to sufferers, as we have seen, such pain is every bit as real as that caused by bodily injury or disease. Psychogenic pain can ruin one's life as surely as the distress of a disfiguring burn or a widespread arthritis. Despite its origins in the psyche, therefore, this sort of rheumatic distress is as much a medical problem as the purely somatic disorders.

But how can a physician determine if rheumatic pain is rooted in physical or psychogenic causes or in a combination of the two? The answer lies in both the expertise of the doctor and the cooperation of the patient. Together, as we saw with respect to fibrositis, doctor and patient analyze body and mind by means of a thorough and forthright medical history.

THE PSYCHE AND RHEUMATIC PAIN

In our discussion of the psyche's role in soft-tissue rheumatism, it will help to categorize the disorders under three distinct headings. The first category is "pure" psychogenic rheumatism, in my experience by far the least common of the three. The second category is actual physical dysfunction caused primarily by psychogenic factors. In the third, physical factors in rheumatism, such as inflammation and tissue injury, generate a psychogenic response.

Pure Psychogenic Rheumatism

By definition, *pure psychogenic rheumatism* refers to musculoskeletal pains that originate in the mind. Again I emphasize the reality of these perceptions. They are as real as any other pains; they create no discernible bodily dysfunction. Where these pains are present, there are no tender muscles, no joint-motion limitation, no joint swelling, and no fever. There are no abnormal laboratory or X-ray studies to explain the presence of the pains. In short, no physical dysfunction corresponds with the pain; the pain itself is the only symptom.

In such cases the forces that create pain are not found in the body at all. Those pain-making forces are what we call emotions or feelings—and, quite specifically, they are *negative* emotions such as fear, hostility, hatred, and so on. Severe neuroses and psychoses and their accompanying emotions can also create pain. How these emotions are translated into pain is unknown, but that they can be is confirmed fact. If you have psychogenic rheumatism and the link between psyche and pain remains unacknowledged, it is inevitable that your doctor's attempts to diagnose the pains will result in a continuous series of expensive examinations, studies, and treatments with disappointing results.

Psychogenic Bodily Dysfunction

In the second category, the same psychogenic factors—emotions and sometimes neuroses and psychoses—cause not only pain but physical manifestations, such as muscle tension with its associated tenderness, stiffness, and at times spasm. Fibrositis is a classic example. In this and other conditions in this category, the muscles are the "target organs" of our emotions, analogous to the blood vessels in high blood pressure, the heart in rapid heartbeats, and the intestines in peptic ulcer or irritable bowel syndrome. We can easily measure blood pressure and heart rates and we can actually see peptic ulcers. As yet, however, we are unable adequately to measure or quantify muscle tension. Since, in our scientific age, we are more prone to accept as real what we can measure, I feel certain that the reluctance in some quarters to view fibrositis as a significant illness is based on a too-facile dismissal of the unmeasurable. Most practicing clinicians, however, have little doubt as to the existence of muscle-tension pains when they see patients who suffer them.

Psychogenic Influences on Pain Perception

In the third category, the disorder begins with a physical cause, namely tissue inflammation or injury, which generates a psychogenic response that increases the pain intensity. Our responses are conditioned by our emotional experiences—our fears, anxieties, expectations and hopes—as well as our present physical condition. Thus tendinitis of the elbow has different meanings to a professional tennis player or violinist than to a sales- or businessperson. It can ruin a career or be a minor nuisance. In a person overwhelmed with tension and stress, a case of tendinitis could be "the last straw" that causes a breakdown in emotional stability. In essence, the same degree of "tennis elbow" can provoke a wide range of concern and pain in different individuals depending on their emotional health. You yourself could probably predict, with a fair degree of accuracy, how people you know well would respond to pain—"stoically" or "oversensitively," in accordance with their emotional experience and personal history.

Cultural Influences

In our discussions of pain up to this point we have neglected another highly significant influence on our psyches: our culture. To a great extent our culture teaches us how great our distress must be before we can consider it real pain worth attending to and, even more important, worth mentioning. Many cultures throughout the world, both ancient and modern, have held the acceptance and stoic endurance of pain and even disfigurement and death to be desirable. In their traditional cultures American Indian boys, for example, are often initiated into manhood by means of a trial of pain.

Children in certain African tribes undergo bodily disfigurement in order to attain social acceptance. Japanese kamikaze pilots during World War II accepted death as a patriotic duty.

Within a culture, too, subgroups have various standards of behavior. Thus it may be acceptable to complain of sore muscles if you're a worker in industry, but it is certainly frowned upon if you're in basic training in the United States Marine Corps.

Our perception of soft-tissue rheumatism pain, like that of any pain, is influenced by complex interrelationships among soma, psyche, and the environment—all molded in turn by our subjective realities. Too often in our search for a simple answer to rheumatic pains we overlook their many-faceted origins. As American writer Henry Adams said, "Simplicity is the most deceitful mistress that ever betrayed man."

CONTROVERSIES AND DILEMMAS

It is safe to say that the more intricate and tangled a problem appears, the more controversies and dilemmas it generates. Psychogenic rheumatism engenders a controversy right from the start: what it should be called. If you suffer from fibrositis, for example, one doctor may call it fibrositis; another, psychogenic rheumatism; another, myofascial pain syndrome; and yet another, myalgic pains. Despite their disagreement, all four physicians may be fully aware of the influences present in the soma-psyche-environment interaction. I have read many articles discussing the same symptoms and the same findings, only to find that this disorder is called by many different names. The result, as you can well imagine, is confusion in the minds of patients and physicians alike.

The basic controversy, I believe, is rooted in semantics. Diseases and disorders have classically been named by different methods. One way is to give a name based on the known or assumed cause—examples are pneumococcal pneumonia, tuberculosis, cerebrovascular occlusion, and psychogenic rheumatism. Another method used, particularly when the cause is unknown or uncertain, bases the name on a given group of symptoms and findings, as in myofascial pain syndrome, polymyalgia rheumatica, and rheumatoid arthritis. The given name may refer to the type of body organ or tissue involved, such as tendinitis, ligamentitis, and bursitis. Yet another method refers to whoever is given credit for discovering or first describing a disease. For instance, ankylosing spondylitis, an inflammatory disease of the spine and other joints, has been called Marie-Strumpell's disease and Von Bechterew's syndrome in addition to many other names.

In disorders where psychogenic and somatic factors interact, the difficulties in naming a problem can be great, since the significance of the contributing factors may vary over time in the same individual. For example, muscle tension pains in a secretary could come from long hours of sitting at a typewriter, from tensions at home or in the office, or both. The time of diagnosis plus the causes the physician feels are paramount might yield a diagnosis of psychogenic rheumatism, muscle tension syndrome, fibrositis, myofascial pain syndrome, or what have you. Given the complexity of the interactions, one might find justification for any of these terms.

We face not only controversy but also dilemma in assessing the role of psychogenic factors in soft-tissue rheumatism. We know that our psyches can play a central role in producing bodily dysfunction and pain, and that disease and pain can lead to psychological disturbances. Therefore, physical disease, pain, limitation of activity, and disability can all increase pain. In the case of a violinist with a severe tennis elbow, the threat of performing poorly at a concert or being unable to complete it would certainly be an understandable cause for fear and anxiety, and these psychological responses in turn could—and would even be likely to—worsen the pain and disability stemming from the condition. The same illness in a professional tennis player or baseball pitcher would be equally as devastating and equally likely to intensify the symptoms. What is the origin of the pain in such a case—soma or psyche? And does it matter which came first, the physical symptoms or the psychological stresses? Indeed it does: To choose a maximally beneficial treatment, we need to know which came first. Let's consider the hypothetical case of Betty, a thirty-four-year-old secretary.

For six months Betty had had muscle pains and stiffness in her upper and lower back, and she was constantly fatigued. She told her doctor that her workload on the job had increased: She was typing more hours a day than before, and she had to carry heavy boxes of records to a storeroom now, a task that used to fall to the mailroom personnel. Still, when her doctor suggested it, Betty denied that she was under any kind of extra tension, protesting that she was happy with her work and with the overtime pay she was earning. The physician diagnosed her as having muscle strain and prescribed a treatment regimen of exercise and aspirin, but these had no effect. He added anti-inflammatory agents and then muscle relaxants, but with no improvement. Betty was growing more agitated with every treatment failure; she asked for stronger painkillers, but her doctor refused, citing the addiction potential as far too dangerous to risk. Betty became disgusted. She went to an orthopedic surgeon, then to an acupuncturist, and then began a search in health food stores in an effort to rid her body of toxins. All her attempts were to no avail. She became fearful and depressed, and turned to alcohol to relieve her anxieties. What on earth was happening to her? she asked herself. Why couldn't medical science find a medicine to get rid of her pain? She grew angry with everyone—her doctor, family, and friends. Nobody understood her, she moaned to herself. As a matter of fact, when she really thought about it, she and her husband had never really gotten along. He never did appreciate her and gave her little or no sympathy when her pains began. Everyone needs some love and kindness, Betty knew, and her boss was willing to provide these. She remembered how he had promised to leave his wife, but of course he never had. She was crushed with disappointment, but she had gotten over it. It was those damn pains, she told herself. They just took the life out of her, that's all. They marked the end of everything good in Betty's life.

Knowing what you do about Betty's condition and some of the rambling thoughts she has had about it, try to pretend for a moment that you are her doctor. You were impressed when she told you that she was putting in many extra hours and doing heavy lifting. You are familiar with the kinds of muscle strains and pains that come from poor posture, and you are adept at treating them. You're quite sure that Betty's complaints are directly related to the new demands of her job, but with what appears to be proper therapy she doesn't improve at all. Thus you begin to suspect she might be under some tension that she hasn't told you about, but she adamantly denies this when you ask her. Disappointed, she leaves your care, and you as well as Betty are left with feelings of frustration.

Now pretend that you are Betty. You know you are under tension and stress but feel certain that something is physically wrong with your body. You are convinced that you have a pinched nerve, vitamin deficiency, or something far worse. You don't believe for a minute that your pain can have anything to do with your problem with your boss—and you'd never even dream of it. If you could just get rid of the pain, you know you can get a handle on the social situation.

Betty's case is typical: Because she is unaware of the power of psychological forces to disrupt our physical beings, she loses the opportunity to treat and eradicate the true cause of her symptoms. Many people resist or refuse to acknowledge that we all have within us unresolved emotional conflicts that can potentially affect our bodies adversely. At times, physical activity or verbal expression are unable to dissipate the energy generated by these conflicts, and the result can be symptoms of musculoskeletal pain. If you suffer pains with such origins, you are surely not alone in the world. It can only be hoped that you and your doctor recognize the possibility that your symptoms have such roots, for without such recognition the cycle is likely to continue.[3]

PATHWAYS TO PAIN RELIEF

Another wrinkle on this situation is of equal importance. Emotional conflict can not only *cause* pain, it can also *prevent its relief*. It is a truism that we are all unique beings, but it's worth noting that our uniqueness extends to our individual ways of handling pain.

An important consideration in treating psychogenic musculoskeletal pain, then, is that our emotions themselves can be obstacles to our own relief. After all, if our emotions produce the pain in the first place, it's possible that we have some heavy stakes in maintaining it. Perhaps, like Betty, we see no way out of the actual conflict or in some way fear its resolution. If this possibility goes unrecognized, these emotional blocks can be impenetrable and frustrating barriers that obstruct our every attempt at pain relief.

Clearly, tearing down these psychic barriers must be the first step in such cases to eradicating the pain, but it is a step that is very difficult to take alone. For this reason, unrestricted mutual cooperation between you and your doctor is an absolute necessity.

The Physician's Role

Remember the first rule of diagnosis: history, history, history—the patient's complete history, that is. Let's look now at what specifically constitutes a patient history and what significance history holds for the diagnosing physician.

The first part of the history is just what the complaints are, how long they have been present, and how they have changed over time. A very important part of that history involves identifying precipitating factors and variables involved in making the symptoms better or worse. As is surely clear by now, these latter factors can arise from anywhere in the soma-psyche-environment relationship.

Where the physician suspects that the psyche may play a role in the symptoms, he or she will probe further into realms the patient often considers unrelated to the problem. The doctor may ask about family, job, boss, hopes, and aspirations. The patient's answers to the questions will help the doctor assess the patient's overall life situation. Ultimately, those answers will play a prominent part in determining the course of the treatment. If the patient's answers are not forthcoming, or are consciously or subconsciously misleading, the doctor's concept of the illness may be wrong and the chosen treatment futile.

The Role of the Patient

We've seen a welcome change recently in the patient's role from that of passive recipient to active participant in the diagnosis and treatment processes. Nowadays people are ever more eager to learn about both disease treatment and preventive medicine, and the general public seems increasingly interested in joining in the fight against illness. Inevitably, therefore, what makes us tick has become increasingly common knowledge, and with this trend has come a growing acceptance of the fact that forces within our psyche may contribute to our misery. More and more patients recognize the need to look inwardly as well as outwardly to find an appropriate pathway to pain relief. These folks are therefore prepared to probe honestly and deeply into the roots of their anxieties, fears, and hostilities. Given this trend, perhaps the day will come when everyone, patient and medical practitioner alike, will routinely consider psyche and environment as well as somatic factors in seeking to eradicate musculoskeletal pains.

Treatment Options

We have seen that probing into the true emotional causes of psychogenic conditions can be painful, but why? Why should we have difficulty telling the truth about our lives to close friends or a trusted doctor? Why do we hold our secrets so tightly, even while we try to divulge them when hoping to reduce our pains?

The answer touches on another protective mechanism that, like pain, can serve as both friend and foe. As we grow from infancy, we develop defense mechanisms and build psychological walls to protect ourselves against hurt. Sometimes these fortress walls around our emotional core grow so solid they do not allow our emotions to escape; in other words, they permit no expression of our innermost truths. Some people have imprisoned their emotions so deeply that they are unaware of the harm they are doing themselves by denying or failing to recognize their innermost reality.

Where the barricade becomes a prison in this way, we must acknowledge the need to break it down, slowly bringing to light the sources of our tensions, stresses, anxieties, fears, and hostilities. Doing this alone—fighting against one's own defense mechanisms—is virtually impossible; a neutral ally is necessary to lend encouragement and support. This person must be not only one with whom we can talk freely but also one who can objectively determine whether or not a relationship exists between the emotions and the illness. In this the ideal candidate is, of course, a doctor who knows us and whom we trust.

If indeed our emotions play a significant part in producing our discomfort, our physician alone may be able to help us deal with the problem. But where the psychological component is complex and challenging, the physician might well advise psychotherapy to supplement the medical course of treatment. Finally, certain self-help methods can help to reduce tensions and anxieties, and in a later chapter we will consider suggestions regarding methods.

6

The Disabling Duo: Polymyalgia Rheumatica and Giant Cell Arteritis

THE GREAT IMITATORS

Mary, age sixty-two, owned a dress shop. For five months she suffered from severe muscular stiffness, restricted movement in her shoulder and hip, swelling of her right knee, and weight loss. Large doses of aspirin and nonsteroidal anti-inflammatory drugs had little effect on her symptoms. She became so disabled that she could neither work nor take care of her home. At first her symptoms and a physical exam yielded a diagnosis of probable rheumatoid arthritis, and she fearfully anticipated years of suffering and disability.

But Mary had polymyalgia rheumatica, which can closely mimic rheumatoid arthritis. With proper therapy she was symptom-free in a matter of days.

In many cases, the diagnosis of rheumatoid arthritis can be made without difficulty and with a high degree of certainty. But rheumatoid arthritis is not without its mimics and imitators. This chapter covers two disorders that are often mistaken for rheumatoid arthritis: polymyalgia rheumatica and giant cell arteritis. These conditions, which can mimic not only arthritis but also cancer, bear a relationship to each other. In fact, the medical evidence connecting polymyalgia rheumatica and giant cell arteritis is so strong that it is difficult to discuss one illness without noting the association to the other.

Polymyalgia rheumatica is characterized primarily by severe muscle ache and stiffness in the shoulder and hip areas. Giant cell arteritis is an inflammatory disease of the arteries resulting in a wide variety of symptoms and findings—headaches, blindness, stroke, heart attack, liver disease, lung disease, skin disorders, jaw cramping, and those indistinguishable from polymyalgia rheumatica, to name just some. Giant cell arteritis is notorious for posing as an infectious disease or for going unrecognized as the cause of its many symptoms.

Syphilis has been traditionally called "the great imitator," owing to the huge diversity of symptoms and physical findings it can produce. Since the advent of penicillin therapy in the 1940s, the incidence of syphilis has sharply declined, and few physicians nowadays see the varied late manifestations of the disease. Instead we are beginning to recognize more frequently the many illnesses produced by the two new "great imitators": polymyalgia rheumatica and giant cell arteritis.

Despite the frequency of their occurrence, and in contrast to rheumatoid arthritis and syphilis, these two related disorders are virtually unknown outside medical circles. They rarely occur in people younger than fifty. Because our population over the age of fifty is steadily growing, and because these disorders generally respond extremely well to treatment, there is an urgency in the need to acquaint the general public with these illnesses. In almost all cases early diagnosis and proper treatment can prevent their severe complications.

Diagnosing polymyalgia rheumatica and giant cell arteritis can be either simple and staightforward or difficult, even when they are suspected by a physician highly skilled in their diagnosis. Both illnesses can be treacherous, and if you might have one of them the services of your physician are not optional, but absolutely essential. You are not a candidate for home diagnosis and treatment if you have one of these conditions; rather, you require medical expertise to prevent potentially catastrophic results.

CASE HISTORIES

Elizabeth, age sixty-seven, was a retired social worker. Her symptoms began insidiously with morning stiffness in her shoulders and hips that loosened up when she moved about. She attributed this pattern to "getting older" and initially was not too concerned. After a few weeks of progressive stiffness and muscle ache, though, she diagnosed herself as having the flu or a virus. She took large doses of vitamin C from a health store but gained no relief. She then visited a chiropractor who diagnosed a "pinched nerve" in her neck and for five weeks treated her with daily spine manipulations. Despite the treatments it became increasingly difficult for her to move about. Her husband had to help her get out of bed in the morning, get dressed, and even get up from chairs whenever she sat down. After three and a half months of suffering, she became convinced she had arthritis and consulted a doctor.

The only significant finding in her physical examination was some limitation of movement of her shoulders and hips. Her physician ordered many laboratory studies and found that she was mildly anemic and had an abnormal sedimentation rate of 88 mm per hour (sedimentation rate is covered in detail later in the chapter). He then referred her to a surgeon who performed a biopsy on a small artery called the temporal artery. The biopsy yielded normal findings. Next, her doctor diagnosed her condition as polymyalgia rheumatica and treated her with an oral medication known as prednisone, a cortisone derivative. The morning after treatment began, Elizabeth found that her symptoms had markedly decreased, and in two days she was able to get out of bed and dress herself without assistance. Within a week she felt normal again.

Elizabeth's symptoms were typical of the syndrome known as polymyalgia rheumatica. An earlier visit to her physician would have saved her months of needless suffering.

Helen, age seventy-three, awoke one morning with severe aching and pain in her neck, shoulder, and hip areas. She was extremely stiff and could hardly get around. After three days she saw her doctor, who ordered the appropriate studies and diagnosed polymyalgia rheumatica. She was treated with prednisone over the course of sixteen months, during which time she felt extremely well. Her doctor administered the prednisone in decreasing dosages, relying on her symptoms and sedimentation rate as a guide to treatment. He asked her to return for a recheck on her sedimentation rate every three months, which she did faithfully for three years.

At this time she made an appointment with her ophthalmologist for her yearly eye examination. By coincidence, on the very morning of her appointment she awakened with a throbbing headache and tenderness over her left temporal area (just above the ear). When she saw her ophthalmologist, he immediately suspected giant cell arteritis and referred her back to her personal doctor. He ordered a biopsy of the temporal artery to be performed that day, and the diagnosis of giant cell arteritis was confirmed. The doctor restarted the prednisone therapy, and Helen's symptoms subsided completely.

Helen's situation was unusual in that typical polymyalgia rheumatica was followed three years later by typical giant cell arteritis. This is not the common pattern, but it underscores the relationship between these two diseases.

At sixty-eight, Herbert was a retired grocer. His symptoms began with "flu-like" discomfort of generalized aching, loss of appetite, and spiking fevers to 103 degrees. After five days of feeling terrible, he saw his doctor. Physically he checked out all right, but his blood studies revealed two abnormalities: a high sedimentation rate of 106 mm per hour and an elevated liver function test known as an "alkaline phosphatase level."

These test results suggested any number of diseases to Herbert's doctor, including an infection or cancer. He hospitalized Herbert for extensive studies that turned up no definite signs of infection or cancer. However, a liver biopsy showed inflammation in a small artery. The doctor diagnosed giant cell arteritis and administered the appropriate dose of prednisone. The symptoms disappeared rapidly, and Herbert made a complete recovery.

Giant cell arteritis is truly "a great imitator." Its initial symptoms may be identical to those of arthritis or polymyalgia rheumatica, but in Herbert's case its mode of appearance initially raised the concern of infection or cancer.

Mary was fifty-eight years old, in good health, and a Christian Scientist. When she was beset by severe muscle stiffness and aching and joint pains in her neck and shoulders, she felt that if she just adhered to her religious principles the symptoms would go away. But Mary became progressively worse. Weight loss and low-grade fever appeared after one month, and after two more weeks she lost vision in her left eye. In another month Mary became confused and forgetful, and was unable to handle her affairs. The court appointed her son as her conservator, and he personally accompanied her to a psychiatrist. The psychiatrist made a diagnosis of senile dementia but insisted that she see a specialist in arthritic diseases because of her severe musculoskeletal complaints, and an ophthalmologist because of her loss of vision. Mary's son made an appointment for her at a university arthritis clinic. After the appropriate studies, the clinic doctor made the correct diagnosis—giant cell arteritis—and instituted treatment immediately. Mary's muscle and joint symptoms subsided, but her confusion persisted and she had no improvement in her vision. Had Mary sought medical assistance earlier, this story would have had a much happier ending.

Bill, age fifty-three, was a traveling salesman who was never in one place too long. His problem began with feeling tired easily and a few aches and pains in his shoulders. Bill's doctor thought Bill might well have fibrositis and prescribed aspirin and then nonsteroidal anti-inflammatory drugs, which had some effect. Shortly afterward Bill left home for a two-month tour selling his merchandise, a stressful ordeal for him. He found that his appetite was decreasing and his muscles were progressively stiffer. In fact, generally he felt terrible. He considered going home but was too busy. He visited three doctors in three cities and told them he had a severe case of fibrositis. All three agreed and refilled his previous prescriptions. By the time he got home, he could hardly move.

Bill's doctor ran some tests and found them all normal except for the sedimentation rate: It had risen from a normal value of 18 to an abnormal value of 76 mm per hour. The doctor revised his diagnosis from fibrositis to polymyalgia rheumatica and treated Bill with the appropriate doses of prednisone. Within five days Bill's symptoms had totally disappeared, and his appetite had returned to normal.

Polymyalgia rheumatica can be an insidious illness—that is, it can begin gradually and get worse over time. For a doctor to suspect fibrositis at the outset of polymyalgia rheumatica is not at all unusual. The course of the two illnesses and their responses to treatment differ sharply, however, so an accurate early diagnosis is essential.

WHAT WE KNOW

Giant Cell Arteritis

The central problem in giant cell arteritis is an inflammation—whose cause in unknown—that can affect arteries in various parts of the body. When arteries become inflamed there is a possibility that the lumens, or channels, of the arteries will become clogged and cause damage or death (infarction) to the tissues they supply with blood and oxygen. For example, if essential arteries to the eye are damaged, blindness results. If arteries to the brain are involved, headaches, confusion, psychoses, or strokes can ensue. If arteries in the tongue become inflamed, parts of the tongue muscle can die.

Where the arteries are only narrowed and blood supply to the tissues is only partially restricted, the damage is less devastating. Narrowing of the arteries to the jaw muscles, for example, can cause cramping in these muscles during chewing—a condition known as *jaw muscle claudication*. When the coronary arteries are narrowed, angina pectoris (pain in the chest area with exertion) may be prominent, and if the arteries are blocked entirely, a myocardial infarction (heart attack) may be the result. Clearly, then, the symptoms of giant cell arteritis vary markedly depending on which arteries are affected by the disease.

As the case studies show, another prominent symptom of giant cell arteritis can be musculoskeletal pain and stiffness identical to that associated with polymyalgia rheumatica. Studies of groups of patients have shown that as many as 60 percent will have the symptoms of polymyalgia rheumatica at some time during their illness. As noted, the symptoms of polymyalgia rheumatica can lead to an erroneous diagnosis of rheumatoid arthritis, and the same possibility applies to giant cell arteritis.

Since the primary disease process in giant cell arteritis is inflammation, the body in this condition reacts as it does to any chronic inflammation—with fever, anemia, weight loss, and a loss of the feeling of well-being. Further, blood studies in patients with giant cell arteritis show changes that can occur in any type of chronic inflammation and are not at all specific to the disease. The sedimentation rate in the blood, however, is usually very high and therefore often suggests the diagnosis. (Sedimentation rate is discussed in detail below.)

The symptoms of giant cell arteritis may come on gradually or strike abruptly. The condition often mimics influenza-like illnesses that seem to go on and on. The variety of this condition's symptoms is truly remarkable.

I have mentioned that giant cell arteritis can mimic the findings of cancer or liver disease. There is an enzyme within the liver called alkaline phosphatase that is also found in small amounts in the blood. When the liver is damaged from any of a host of causes—such as cancer that has spread to the liver, various forms of liver disease, or blockage of the liver ducts—this enzyme leaks from the liver cells and becomes elevated in the blood serum. The same type of abnormal liver tests are found when giant cell arteritis is present. If the arteritis is undiagnosed, the liver abnormalities may be suspected as being those of cancer or primary liver disease.

Giant cell arteritis was recognized as a disease years before an effective treatment was found. For this reason we know quite a bit about what is called the "natural history of the disease"—or what happens if it's not treated. Initially the disease was thought to be a "self-limiting" one that would run its course in six months; later, however, it became clear that although the disease often does eventually limit itself, it can remain active for many years. Fortunately it was discovered that in most cases cortisone derivatives in controlled doses end the ravages of the disease in a matter of days.

To this day, the cause of giant cell arteritis remains a mystery. Medical investigators have probed many areas, searching for infectious agents, immunologic processes, or genetic susceptibilities that might explain the affliction. Despite all efforts, though, the causes of the disease remain hidden. Perhaps we should count ourselves doubly fortunate, therefore, that we have managed to find a successful treatment for giant cell arteritis in spite of our ignorance of its inciting cause or causes.

Polymyalgia Rheumatica

The main symptoms of polymyalgia rheumatica are aching, pain, and feelings of stiffness in the muscles in the areas of the neck, shoulders, and hips that persist for long periods of time—often for many years. Pains around the joints occur and often mimic those of arthritis. In addition, the patient might suffer weight loss and fever. And, as with giant cell arteritis, the sedimentation rate in the blood is almost always abnormally high.

Where polymyalgia rheumatica is present, blood studies show the nonspecific findings of inflammation found in giant cell arteritis, although it is usually less severe. Again, polymyalgia rheumatica can also be associated with abnormal liver function tests suggestive of cancer. Still, in pure polymyalgia rheumatica, no consistent abnormalities have been found in any tissue of the body that account for the severity of the symptoms. Untreated, the syndrome can wreak havoc for years. Treated, its symptoms can be halted in days.

You may have noticed that I have referred to giant cell arteritis as a disease and to polymyalgia rheumatica as a syndrome. There are technical differences between a disease and a syndrome. A *disease* is a specific clinical condition that can be clearly set apart from a normal state or from other pathological entities. A *syndrome* is not so clear-cut; it consists of a group of signs and symptoms that characterize a particular *type* of illness or disorder. Giant cell arteritis is associated with specific pathologic findings—of inflammation of arteries—and is thus a disease. Polymyalgia rheumatica has not yet yielded any specific findings, so the collection of symptoms that characterize it are referred to as a syndrome. A "cold," for example, is not a disease but a syndrome, since the same symptoms can be caused by different organisms or an allergy. Thus it is with polymyalgia rheumatica: The set of symptoms may have one or any number of causes; we do not know.

Those at Risk

Giant cell arteritis and polymyalgia rheumatica rarely strike anyone under the age of fifty. The incidences of both conditions gradually increase with increasing age, and both are most frequently seen in people over seventy. Also, for unknown reasons that might eventually yield some insight into causes, both disorders strike women more often than men—a factor they have in common with rheumatoid arthritis. The population at risk for both illnesses is a large one and has been growing faster than the overall population of the United States. The United States Census Bureau figures tell us that in 1970 there were 49.7 million in the United States over the age of fifty (constituting 24.45 percent of the total), while in 1980 the number was 60 million (26 percent of the total).

Studies done in Olmsted County, Minnesota, by the Mayo Clinic give us an idea of the number of people who could be affected by these disorders. The study of the prevalence of giant cell arteritis covers the period 1970–1974, and that of polymyalgia rheumatica covers 1970–1979.[1,2] The results indicate that polymyalgia rheumatica is three to four times more common than giant cell arteritis. Every year in the United States giant cell arteritis strikes an estimated 10,000 people, and 72,000 people are now suffering from the disease. Every year 29,000 people are struck with polymyalgia rheumatica, and as many as 300,000 are now afflicted with that disorder. The Mayo Clinic compared polymyalgia rheumatica with rheumatoid arthritis, the commonest chronic inflammatory rheumatic disease, and found that the former was actually catching up with the latter in those over fifty years of age: "Annual incidence . . . approaches that of patients presenting with definite or classical rheumatoid arthritis" was how the clinic put it. Further, the clinic stated that "polymyalgia rheumatica is a relatively common disease in this age group." I might add that other studies done on smaller population sizes suggest these disorders might occur even more frequently than the Olmsted County studies indicate.

With regard to giant cell arteritis, it is interesting that it has been reported mainly in people of European ancestry. The disease occurs in blacks, but far less often. This fact, along with a number of family studies, suggests that genetic factors might be an important contributing cause. Reassuringly, there has been no significant association of giant cell arteritis with cancer.

Medical Sleuthing

It is intriguing to speculate on how long the disorders of giant cell arteritis and polymyalgia rheumatica have plagued human beings. Archaeological studies of bones have given us evidence of arthritis in prehistoric people. The ravages of time on soft tissues, in contrast, leave us no clues as to when giant cell arteritis and polymyalgia rheumatica first made their appearances. Our knowledge stems from the observations of the medical sleuths, the alert physicians who first chronicled these exotic disorders and gradually assembled a picture of them.

The story begins in England in 1890 with a description by Dr. Jonathan Hutchinson of the headache of a Mr. Rumbold, the father of a porter at the London Hospital. Mr. Rumbold could not tolerate wearing his hat because of inflamed and tender temporal arteries (these lie under the skin in the area just above the ears).[3] Dr. Hutchinson assumed that the cause of this problem was a tight hatband. The real cause, giant cell arteritis, went unrecognized by most physicians until 1932 when Drs. Horton, Magath, and Brown published the classical description of the disease in the *Proceedings of the Staff Meetings of the Mayo Clinic*.[4] Six years later, in 1938, blindness was found to be a complication of the disease.

The growing awareness of giant cell arteritis yielded the discovery that any medium- or large-sized artery in the body could be involved—often those deep within the body and relatively inaccessible to easy diagnosis. Slowly, the hidden and varied manifestations of the finding came to light. Many disorders that were previously diagnosed as arthritis, "probable viruses," "fevers of undetermined origin," strokes due to hardening of the arteries, "senility," and psychoses were proven to be due to giant cell arteritis. The list of symptoms commonly misdiagnosed is long and still growing. In 1983 alone, more than four hundred articles appeared in medical journals throughout the world describing various aspects of giant cell arteritis.

Because of the initial findings of inflamed temporal arteries, the disease was initially known by the name temporal arteritis. It was later found that other arteries in the head and within the brain could be involved, and the term cranial arteritis came into vogue. A frequent but not inevitable finding in the inflamed arteries was the presence of large cells with many nuclei, termed *giant cells* (visible only under the microscope). Eventually the term giant cell arteritis became most acceptable, since this name does not suggest that the disease is limited only to the temporal areas or the head. It is interesting and perhaps fitting that even today many articles in the medical literature refer to giant cell arteritis as Horton's disease, in honor of the physician who first described it substantively.

Giant cell arteritis was clearly defined as a disease in 1932, twenty-five years before polymyalgia rheumatica first gained acceptance as anything but a vague musculoskeletal problem affecting the elderly. It was only after 1957 that the link between these two became evident.

Now let us shift our attention to the incidents surrounding the emergence of polymyalgia rheumatica as an important soft-tissue rheumatic syndrome. Credit for the first description of this syndrome is given to a Dr. Bruce, who in 1888, two years before Dr. Hutchinson's description of what we now call giant cell arteritis, reported a case of "senile rheumatic gout."[5] By the 1940s and 1950s, descriptions consistent with polymyalgia rheumatica were reported in the medical literature under a variety of names—such as fibrositis, rheumatoid syndrome of the elderly, myalgic syndrome, anarthritic rheumatoid disease (rheumatoid arthritis without arthritis), and the imposing one of periarthrosis humeroscapularis.

The name that has gained the greatest acceptance in the English literature, polymyalgia rheumatica, was first suggested in 1957.[6] The term is descriptive of the disorder—*poly* meaning many, *myalgia* meaning muscle pains, and *rheumatica* meaning of rheumatic origin. The French, by the way, generally prefer the term *pseudopolyarthrite rhizomelique,* meaning a false arthritis of many joints—again highlighting the point that this syndrome is not basically an arthritic one.

Because the symptoms of polymyalgia rheumatica are often vague, the syndrome was slow to gain acceptance as an entity. The medical profession's inability to come up with a specific finding or "test" for it made many physicians leery of even giving a name to what they considered some very nonspecific complaints. The doubters, I might add, played an important role in describing polymyalgia rheumatica, since they forced the believers to be more specific in defining the syndrome. In fact, as late as 1966, in one of the major textbooks on arthritis, polymyalgia rheumatica was given only two paragraphs in the chapter on fibrositis.[7] The contributing author described it as "a clinical syndrome struggling for recognition as a separate entity." He further stated that "the proponents of the syndrome of 'polymyalgia rheumatica' may have selected those elderly patients with fibrositis who happen to have a high sedimentation rate, arbitrarily gave their illness a new pseudospecific name. . . ." Having trained in rheumatology prior to 1966, I can fully appreciate his skepticism.

However, as more and more clinical studies from major medical centers all over the world poured into the medical literature, it became apparent that there surely was an entity that we could call polymyalgia rheumatica. Now we know its symptoms—but what is it? Is it just a collection of symptoms, or is it a disease in its own right? Can it appear alone, or can the symptoms occur with another disease? Many questions remain unanswered, but some are currently being addressed.

During the 1960s some patients with polymyalgia rheumatica were found to have inflammation of the temporal arteries identical to that in giant cell arteritis. This was the first link discovered between the two diseases. Next, reports came in of disorders typical of polymyalgia rheumatica but accompanied by swelling of the knees or joints of the wrists, fingers, or clavicles, causing confusion with rheumatoid arthritis.

It is now apparent that a strong link exists between polymyalgia rheumatica and giant cell arteritis. The two are so close, in fact, that many investigators believe they are not separate entities but one disease with a spectrum of possible manifestations.

HOW THEY ARE DIAGNOSED

If you have any of the symptoms discussed in this chapter, you may be asking yourself how to diagnose giant cell arteritis or polymyalgia rheumatica, but you really can't diagnose these conditions. You should know about them because you may *suspect* you have one or the other. I hope I have convinced you to see a doctor quickly if you do have such suspicions. If the possibility is not borne out, no harm will have been done. If you turn out to be right, you may have saved yourself a lot of grief and misery.

Furthermore, if you are being treated for an illness that you suspect may be one of the two under discussion, don't hesitate to raise the possibility with your doctor. It's unlikely that any physician would be offended by such a suggestion. During my internship I was asked to see a woman of sixty-two who had been diagnosed as psychotic by a psychiatrist. When I walked into the room I saw a lethargic, obese woman with a sallow complexion. The first thing she said to me, in a low and slow voice (typical of thyroid hormone lack), was, "I wonder if I have bad thyroid function." After hearing her voice, I felt certain that she was correct—and the lab tests proved that she was—but she wasn't even sure where she had gotten the idea. Most doctors have had similar experiences, impressing them with the notion that patients can indeed often intuit accurate diagnoses.

In discussing diagnoses, it's important to reiterate the fact that both giant cell arteritis and polymyalgia rheumatica can mimic and imitate arthritis, muscle diseases, fibrositis, and even psychiatric conditions. In addition, giant cell arteritis can superficially appear to be a disease of the eyes, brain, heart, lungs, or other organs, and it can masquerade as an infection or cancer as well. Both can be treacherous, painful, and disabling diseases. On the positive side I want to emphasize that in both conditions months and even years of symptoms can often be reversed in days and that potentially serious effects on the body can be prevented. The fact that these disorders are indeed treatable makes early diagnosis as crucial as it is.

But suppose you do go to your doctor and say, "What do you think? Could I have one of those illnesses called giant cell arteritis or polymyalgia rheumatica?" What will the physician do to test the possibilities? Since polymyalgia rheumatica is the more common of the two disorders, we'll begin with that.

Polymyalgia Rheumatica

Recall my insistence on the crucial role the patient's history plays in the art of diagnosis. Polymyalgia rheumatica takes such a distinctive course that it must be considered a primary possibility when its symptoms are present. As noted previously, the muscle stiffness and aching of this disorder occur mainly in the muscles around the shoulders and hips, and those joints often seem to give the feeling that arthritis is present—which can account for the common confusion between polymyalgia rheumatica and arthritis. The stiffness may loosen with activity, only to return after sitting or sleeping. If the disease progresses, weight loss, fatigue, and fever may be present.

After noting the history of the illness and your general medical history, your physician will then do a physical examination of your body. If polymyalgia rheumatica is present, he or she may find nothing abnormal at all. On the other hand, the exam might confirm limited motion in your hip or shoulder joints.

Following the history and the physical examination, the doctor will have in mind a list of possible diagnoses—what are called the *differential diagnoses*. Your symptoms may raise the question of many possibilities, including (but not limited to) fibrositis, rheumatoid arthritis, hypothyroidism (low thyroid function), other muscle disorders, infection, anxiety, and even malignancy. The doctor will then order the blood tests and X rays necessary to distinguish your problem from all those possible.

Polymyalgia rheumatica itself causes no abnormal X-ray findings, but blood studies may reveal one or more abnormalities. As noted repeatedly, the one that is consistently present in polymyalgia rheumatica is a high sedimentation rate. Since the sedimentation rate plays an extremely important role in the diagnosis and treatment of this disorder, a more detailed explanation of it is in order.

In performing the sedimentation rate test, the practitioner draws blood with a needle and syringe and adds a small amount of an anticoagulant to prevent the blood from clotting. A small amount of the blood is then transferred with a pipette to a long, thin, hollow calibrated glass tube and allowed to stand vertically for one hour. During this time the formed elements of the blood—the red and white cells and the platelets—slowly settle down or "sediment," leaving the clear yellow plasma above. The *sedimentation rate* is the number of millimeters (mm) that these formed elements fall in one hour. If, for example, there are 30 mm of clear plasma present at the top of the tube, this means that the formed elements of the blood have fallen or sedimented 30 mm. Hence, the sedimentation rate is 30 mm per hour.

Sedimentation readings considered normal are up to 10 mm per hour in men and 20 mm per hour in women. In reality, however, normal rates may be a little higher and tend to increase with increasing age.

Abnormal sedimentation rates are not specific for any disease, since they may be affected by various factors. Inflammation in the body from any cause—for example, bacterial or viral infections—are a primary cause of elevated sed rates. Many forms of arthritis and diseases that are linked with immunological abnormalities such as systemic lupus erythematosus also cause elevated rates. Large amounts of abnormal proteins in the blood, as in the blood malignancy disorder of multiple myeloma, can also raise the rates. Thus, although a high sedimentation rate signals the presence of any number of disorders, it cannot serve as a diagnosis in any of them.

In polymyalgia rheumatica, the sedimentation rate is usually above 50 mm per hour, and rates over 100 mm per hour are not uncommon. Again, a high sedimentation rate in this test may be the *only* abnormality found after extensive studies have been done. However, other blood studies may show some mild-to-moderate anemia (a low red blood cell count) or even some liver function abnormalities, such as the alkaline phosphatase, as previously described regarding giant cell arteritis.

If you have an elevated sedimentation rate and the total picture points to the diagnosis of polymyalgia rheumatica, your physician might order one more study—a biopsy of the temporal artery. The point here is to determine with more certainty whether or not giant cell arteritis is also present.

In some cases of polymyalgia rheumatica, one or more joints may be swollen—particularly the knees or wrists. In this situation it may be difficult to differentiate the disorder from rheumatoid arthritis. This problem has generated much controversy in rheumatologic circles, and the criteria for resolving the question are still in dispute.[8]

Giant Cell Arteritis

We shift our attention now to that other troublemaker—giant cell arteritis. The diagnosis of this condition might be simple and straightforward; conversely, it can tax the ingenuity of even the most experienced clinicians, even when they suspect its presence. The reason is that the inflamed arteries can be clearly apparent or hidden deeply within the body.

The "classical" presentation of giant cell arteritis—severe headaches, fever, and swollen and tender temporal arteries—gives no great diagnostic problem. However, fever, aching, and a high sedimentation rate can be caused by any number of diseases. Sudden blindness has many causes, too, as does illness associated with abnormal liver function studies. It is beyond the scope of this book to mention all the disorders that giant cell arteritis can mimic.

Often, the first clue that giant cell arteritis is present is an extremely high sedimentation rate. It tends to be higher than that found in polymyalgia rheumatica—often above 80 mm per hour and not uncommonly as high as 120 mm per hour. Again, the sedimentation rate diagnoses nothing, but it is a clue and a very important one.

The most accessible and frequently involved arteries in the body are the temporal arteries. These lie under the scalp just above the ears and are easy to feel. Sections of these arteries can be surgically removed for study with no apparent effect on the blood supply to any tissue. If they are affected by giant cell arteritis, the typical findings are inflammation and "giant cells" with many nuclei. The disease may affect only one of the arteries, only part of an artery, or other than a temporal artery. The disease often seems to be playing hide and seek with the physician. The stakes are high, however, and the seeking prior to an accurate diagnosis may involve intensive study.

Sometimes extensive tests fail to reveal the existence of giant cell arteritis even when the examining doctor is fairly sure it is present. What then? At this point the doctor might decide to give you a trial of treatment. If the diagnosis is correct, the response is likely to be dramatic—disappearance of muscle aches and pains, relief of fever or headache, a return of the feeling of well-being, all in a matter of days.

As I have said, although you cannot make a definite diagnosis of giant cell arteritis yourself, you can suspect it. When it is indeed present and is accompanied by headaches and swollen temporal arteries, the risk of sudden blindness is high, and prompt medical intervention is essential.

TWO DISEASES—OR ONE?

It all used to seem simple enough—polymyalgia rheumatica and giant cell arteritis were two distinct disorders. That was before biopsies of the temporal arteries in cases of polymyalgia rheumatica showed that some had signs of inflammation typical of giant cell arteritis. Also, many patients with giant cell arteritis have symptoms of polymyalgia rheumatica at some time during their disease. Are they two diseases, one disease and a syndrome, different aspects of one disease—or what?

We simply don't know. We do not yet have all the pieces of the puzzle and do not fully understand the link between these two conditions. However, we do know that they can be treated, and we turn now to an overview of treatment methods.

TREATMENT

Polymyalgia rheumatica and giant cell arteritis are linked in more ways than one. They are both effectively treated by a medication that does not cure either disorder. A contradictory statement? By no means.

The medication most commonly used to treat these disorders is prednisone, a derivative of the hormone cortisone that was first isolated from the cortex of the adrenal gland. Prednisone too is a hormone, one of the many compounds we refer to as *steroids*. It is a potent suppressor of inflammation and has been used beneficially to treat almost every rheumatic disease known. Unfortunately, the adverse side effects of this medication have frightened some people, leaving them with no appreciation for the beneficial effects of the substance. The story of cortisone and its derivatives is told in detail in a later chapter, but a few words about prednisone are in order here.

Prednisone has many effects on bodily function—some good and some bad. As a medication it is used most often to suppress inflammation. It is the "gold standard" by which all other anti-inflammatory medications can be measured. When used appropriately, it can be an almost miraculous reliever of many illnesses that cause misery and disability. Proper doses of prednisone will rapidly bring practically all cases of polymyalgia rheumatica and giant cell arteritis under control. But let me emphasize the words "bring under control," as opposed to the word "cure."

The two disorders we're considering here are "self-limited diseases," which means they last for a certain length of time and then seem to "burn out" by themselves. Unfortunately, if left untreated they may not burn out for years—and then only after taking a serious toll. Also, recurrences are not unknown. For example, many years after polymyalgia has subsided, giant cell arteritis may appear.

Treatment with proper doses of prednisone, given daily and orally in pill form, will decrease the inflammation and symptoms in a matter of days. Other derivatives of cortisone may be as effective, but prednisone is generally used, since it is effective, has fewer side effects than some other derivatives, and is inexpensive and readily available. No other class of drugs other than cortisone and its derivatives has been shown to be as effective in treating these disorders.

The amount of prednisone required to control polymyalgia rheumatica and giant cell arteritis varies from person to person, and also varies according to which of the two is at issue. Generally, polymyalgia rheumatica requires smaller doses than giant cell arteritis. Because the situations vary, I can only give a rough guide as to what to expect regarding drug treatment.

For polymyalgia rheumatica, an initial dose of 10 to 20 milligrams (mg) a day may be needed to suppress all the symptoms. For giant cell arteritis, 60 mg or more may be required initially. Your physician will attempt to reduce the dose as rapidly as good medical judgment permits.

Prednisone is used to suppress what is called "the activity" of the disease, thus suppressing muscle and joint aching, pain, and stiffness. Even more important, in the case of giant cell arteritis prednisone will suppress and relieve the inflammation of the arteries and can prevent the blindness and other serious consequences of the disease. If the dose of prednisone is too small, the inflammation and symptoms will reappear. The trick in treatment is to give enough prednisone to control the disorder but no more than is needed at the time. Again, prednisone does not cure; it suppresses.

As time passes, even under treatment polymyalgia rheumatica and giant cell arteritis will slowly run their courses and "burn out." During this process the doctor will slowly decrease the amount of prednisone. But how does the doctor know when to decrease the prednisone dosage, since the symptoms are suppressed? Again, the blood sedimentation rate serves as a useful guide. When the activity of the disorders is suppressed, the sedimentation rate falls, usually to normal limits. If the prednisone is reduced too rapidly, the first sign of the increased inflammation is usually a rise in the sedimentation rate. Such an elevation would alert the doctor that the prednisone dosage should be increased. From this you can see the importance of visiting a doctor frequently during the course of the treatment and of possibly submitting to studies at regular intervals depending on the progress of the disease.

One last word about prednisone: It is a potent medication with potential deleterious side effects. I encourage you to read about it in "The Role of Your Doctor." Usually the dose can be successfully reduced to a point where these side effects are minimal or nonexistent. In treating such serious disorders as we have discussed, the choice is often between some possible side effects or pain, misery, disability, possible blindness, or even death. Personally, I would take the prednisone.

One point remains to be made about polymyalgia rheumatica. Some experienced physicians feel that mild cases of this disorder can be effectively treated with aspirin or one of the nonsteroidal anti-inflammatory drugs. Most doctors feel, however, that small doses of prednisone are far more effective and pose little risk to the patient. If you have been diagnosed as having polymyalgia rheumatica and have wondered whether your doctor's treatment is aggressive enough, it is useful for you to know that some controversy exists and that another doctor might be more inclined to treat with prednisone.

7

The Pinnacle of Pain: The Reflex Sympathetic Dystrophy

[A] painful swelling of the joints . . . may attack any or all articulations of a member. . . . Once fully established, it keeps the joint stiff and sore for weeks or months. . . . Were we asked to state in what essential respect these lesions differ from subacute rheumatic disease . . . we should certainly be at some loss to discern a difference.

—Dr. Silas Weir Mitchell, 1864[1]

John, a thirty-six-year-old electrical engineer, was varnishing his living room floor when he slipped and mildly sprained his left ankle. He wrapped the ankle in an elastic bandage, bought himself a cane, and hobbled around for two days. On the second day his ankle and foot became more swollen, hot, and excruciatingly painful—so sensitive that even the pressure of his sock on the skin was intolerable. John's next line of self-therapy was to increase his already large intake of highballs, but this strategy yielded little success. Unable to sleep because of the pain, he went to his doctor. John suspected that he had an acute attack of gout, and his physician agreed. His laboratory tests showed a high serum uric acid level, a finding consistent with gout. The X ray revealed no evidence of a fracture.

John was treated adequately for gout, but he got no better. Large doses of codeine barely dulled his pain. The skin over his ankle and foot turned hot to the touch at one time and cold and perspiring the next. Every movement of the ankle caused unbearable pain. John's physician was perplexed and discussed the situation with a few other doctors. One suggested the possibility of reflex sympathetic dystrophy, which was ultimately confirmed. The appropriate therapy was begun, and John had a slow but complete recovery.

It's clear by now that the list of soft-tissue rheumatic diseases capable of imitating arthritis is a long one. This list would not be complete without adding that painful, perplexing, and enigmatic condition known as reflex sympathetic dystrophy and its associated symptoms of causalgia. The first major study of these conditions was done during the American Civil War by an astute Union Army surgeon, Dr. Silas Weir Mitchell. Dr. Mitchell was a fascinating gentleman, and we'll return to him later.

Although not as common as the other disorders discussed in this book, reflex sympathetic dystrophy warrants wider attention for a variety of reasons. The most important reason is familiar by now: Early recognition and treatment are the essential ingredients of a successful recovery. If reflex sympathetic dystrophy goes unrecognized and untreated, it can lead to a permanently useless and disabled hand, foot, or leg, along with severe and persistent pain. The fact that this disorder is not as common as the other soft-tissue rheumatic ones makes it all the easier to miss and therefore all the more important that we learn to distinguish it from the many bodily disturbances that initially appear to be arthritis.

Reflex sympathetic dystrophy is a study in bodily functions gone awry. Often when it develops it follows an injury—major or trivial—but sometimes it is independent of any apparent trauma. Instead of a normal healing response to an instance of tissue damage, the body responds with an almost volcano-like surging of pain and swelling in one or more limbs. Most instances of reflex sympathetic dystrophy follow major trauma and are seen primarily by general surgeons, orthopedic surgeons, and neurosurgeons, all of whom are familiar with its features. When the condition follows minor injuries or appears with no apparent cause, it is most likely to be seen by family practice physicians or internists, who quite often consider it to be some other disorder initially, such as arthritis or infection. Because treatment of reflex sympathetic dystrophy differs markedly from that of arthritis or infection, an early error in diagnosis can lead to ineffective therapy.

The treatment of reflex sympathetic dystrophy decidedly *does not* fall into the "do it yourself" category. The services of a physician, and often of a physical therapist as well, are absolutely essential. This being the case, you might well ask yourself why you ought to bother learning about this condition at all. There are two good reasons. First, this disorder presents enough clues to allow you to suspect its presence when the symptoms occur together. If you think you have reflex sympathetic dystrophy, suggest the possibility to your doctor. You could be wrong, but if you are right you will have done yourself a great service. Second, if you have been diagnosed as having reflex sympathetic dystrophy, your increased knowledge of the disease will help you understand the rationale of the treatment and allow you to participate more actively in your recovery.

DEFINING THE TERMS

At this point a description of three separate but interrelated disorders will contribute to an understanding of reflex sympathetic dystrophy. These three conditions compose the category we call the *sympathetic dystrophies*. The first, *causalgia,* is a "syndrome" that is considered to be a type of reflex sympathetic dystrophy that can occur after nerve injuries are sustained. (Again, the term *syndrome* refers to a group of signs and symptoms that characterize a specific disease or abnormal condition.) The second is *reflex sympathetic dystrophy,* a syndrome with many causes. The third is *Sudeck's atrophy,* a condition that can result when reflex sympathetic dystrophy goes untreated or in those rare instances when it responds poorly to treatment. Let's begin with causalgia, since historically it was the first to be described.

Causalgia

The term *causalgia* was first used shortly after the American Civil War by Dr. S. W. Mitchell, at the suggestion of his close friend, Professor Robley Dunglison.[2] It means burning pain and is derived from the Greek word *kausos,* meaning burning heat, and the suffix *-algia,* meaning pain. Causalgia is a type of neuralgia, which is acute pain radiating along a nerve and its branches. The pain itself is severe and persistent; characteristically, the sufferer feels either a burning or throbbing quality along the course of the nerve involved and in the surrounding tissues. The discomfort is accentuated by environmental stimuli, as when the skin is touched, when the temperature changes, even when someone walks across the floor sending vibrations through the room. In keeping with our understanding of psychogenic pain perception, causalgia can also be accentuated by emotional stimuli, such as anxiety or depression. Visible manifestations of the syndrome are skin changes at the involved area: The skin can become cold, cyanotic (blue from lack of oxygen), perspiring, and glossy.

Causalgia most commonly occurs after a partial injury to a major nerve, such as that caused by a bullet or other high-velocity missile. This is called major causalgia. It may also follow trauma without nerve injury and be less severe than that of major causalgia. This used to be referred to as "minor causalgia" but is now more commonly called post-traumatic sympathetic dystrophy. Causalgia is considered to be a form of reflex sympathetic dystrophy, but the term is most likely to be used when there is definite evidence of a nerve injury.

Reflex Sympathetic Dystrophy

The term *reflex sympathetic dystrophy* refers to an array of symptoms and physical findings. Central to the condition is burning pain that can be identical to that of causalgia. Also involved are signs of an abnormally functioning sympathetic nervous system: swelling, pain, and abnormal temperature changes in a hand, forearm, foot, or leg. These are thought to be due to the results of *dystrophy,* which means a disorder caused by defective nutrition or metabolism. We now know that the joints themselves may be involved in some cases, suggesting that at times a mild form of arthritis may actually be present along with the other findings.

Reflex sympathetic dystrophy can manifest itself following any number of bodily disorders—sprains, burns, tendinitis, fractures, abdominal surgery, and even heart attacks. In the case of a heart attack (myocardial infarction), the reflex sympathetic dystrophy may express itself as what is called the *shoulder-hand syndrome.* In this disorder the shoulder becomes painful and its motion limited, suggesting a tendinitis or a frozen shoulder. These initial symptoms are followed by pain and swelling in the hand, suggesting an acute arthritis such as rheumatoid arthritis or gout. Most often it is the left rather than the right side that is involved. At times, however, as noted earlier, reflex sympathetic dystrophy is not associated with an apparent injury or underlying disease, and in such a case it closely resembles an acute arthritic condition. For practitioners relatively unfamiliar with reflex sympathetic dystrophy, such an instance can easily yield an erroneous diagnosis of arthritis.

Sudeck's Atrophy

In 1900, under the title "Of an Acute Inflammatory Bone Atrophy," Dr. P. Sudeck described a condition consistent with reflex sympathetic dystrophy in which the result was stiffness of the joints, atrophy (wasting or diminishing) of an extremity, and severe thinning of the bones.[3] The describer's name was attached to the condition, and we know the disorder now as Sudeck's atrophy. This extremely disabling condition can result when reflex sympathetic dystrophy remains untreated, but it is almost totally preventable when the dystrophy is recognized and treated in its earliest phases.

THE CAUSES

Causalgia, reflex sympathetic dystrophy, and Sudeck's atrophy are all related disorders sharing the same underlying cause or causes. They are so closely related, in fact, that the terms are often used interchangeably (though to do so is to be imprecise).

However, though we know that these conditions have similar causes, precisely what these causes are is a matter of ongoing controversy. We know that the illnesses seem to involve two distinct sets of nerves: the sensory nerves (the nerves that carry sensation from the skin, muscles, tendons, and the like to the spinal cord and brain) and the nerves that make up the *autonomic nervous system,* particularly its subsystem known as the *sympathetic nervous system.* The nerves in this system relate to *autonomic*—or automatic—functions, over which we have very little conscious control. They dictate blood flow to the skin, muscles, intestines, and other organs, and are involved in such functions as perspiring, changes in pupil size, and reproduction. An important function of the sympathetic nervous system is controlling the release of adrenaline at the ends of the nerve fibers. Adrenaline, also known as epinephrine, is also produced by the medulla, or inner part of the adrenal gland. It has many effects, one of which is to cause constriction of certain blood vessels.

How does injury to these nerves result in the symptoms associated with the sympathetic dystrophies? When body tissues are damaged, the sensory nerves "sense" the injury and carry the signals back to the brain via the spinal cord. At various points in this complex switchboard where reflex sympathetic dystrophy occurs, these signals somehow connect to and incite the sympathetic nervous system into a severe overreaction. The sympathetic activity increases the production of adrenaline, changes the blood flow, and alters local metabolism and nutrition, all effects that result in pain, loss of motion, swelling, and skin and bone changes. These changes in turn cause more signals of injury and perpetuate the cycle. It is also possible that the disorder may cause a heightened reaction to adrenaline.

The theoretical thinking on the possible causes of the sympathetic dystrophies is complex and incomplete. For our purposes, what is important to remember is that the process involves an interreaction, or *reflex,* between the sensory nerves and the *sympathetic* nervous system, and that it causes *dystrophy* (defective nutrition or metabolism) in the affected tissues. Hence the name *reflex sympathetic dystrophy.*

Bitter Lessons of the Civil War

We know that knowledge often begins in hardship. The ravages of the American Civil War, for example, enabled Dr. Silas Weir Mitchell (1829–1914) to recognize and vividly describe the syndrome of causalgia in the course of studying peripheral nerve injuries.[1,4]

Mitchell was a prolific writer on many subjects, including nerve injuries, physiology, psychology, doctor/patient relationships, and historical aspects of the Civil War. His writings included novels, poems, historical romances, orations, magazine articles, and children's stories. Medically, he was also concerned about the effects of excess mental exertion on the nervous system, heart, stomach, and other organs. Although he did not use the terms *stress, tension,* and *burn-out,* in familiar use today, he was well aware of and warned against the detrimental effects of excess "brain labor," "brain tire," and pursuit of the "Dollar Devil."[5]

Before Mitchell published his work on causalgia, a few reports had found their way into the medical literature, but Mitchell's descriptions were the first to treat the condition thoroughly. Not only did they establish the seriousness of causalgia as a separate entity, but in the large view they detailed one of the many tragic consequences of what today is called *conventional warfare:*

Usually the pains from nerve hurts are either aching, shooting, or burning, or perhaps all three at once. Looking carefully through my notes as to this point, I find that in a considerable proportion of gunshot wounds of nerves there is principally burning pain, or at least that this is the prominent symptom, while in slight injuries of nerves from compression or contusion, the other forms of pain are most apt to prevail.

Perhaps few persons who are not physicians can realize the influence which long-continued and unendurable pain may have upon both body and mind. . . . Under such torments the temper changes, the most amiable grow irritable, the soldier becomes a coward, and the stongest man is scarcely less nervous than the most hysterical girl. . . .

The intensity varies from the most trivial burning to a state of torture . . . until the general health is seriously affected. The part itself is not alone subject to an intense burning sensation but becomes exquisitely hyperaesthetic, so that a touch or a tap of the finger increases the pain. Exposure to the air is avoided by the patient with a care which seems absurd, and most of the bad cases keep the hand constantly wet, finding relief in the moisture rather than in the coolness of the application. Two of these sufferers carried a bottle of water and a sponge, and never permitted the part to become dry for a moment. As the pain increases, the general sympathy becomes more marked. The temper changes and grows irritable, the face becomes anxious and has a look of weariness and suffering. The sleep is restless . . . the rattling of a newspaper, a breath of air, the step of another across the ward, the vibrations caused by a military band, or the shock of the feet in walking, gives rise to increase of pain.[6]

Mitchell interprets a soldier's description of his causalgic pain: "It is as if a rough bar of iron were thrust to and fro through the knuckles, a red-hot iron placed at the junction of the palm and thenar eminence, with a heavy weight on it, and the skin was being rasped off my finger-ends."[7]

As to treatment, Mitchell says, "A vast number of means

were tried to ease or cure causalgia, but the one essential for comfort was the use of water-dressings which were unceasingly renewed, the sufferers carrying a bottle of water and a sponge and keeping the part covered. I have never known a man afflicted with causalgia who did not learn very soon the use of this agent, and I never knew one who could be induced to exchange it for any other permanent dressing."[8]

We tend to think of the ancient art of acupuncture as having been relatively recently introduced into Western medicine. Mitchell's comments on this subject are of interest: "Of acupuncture in traumatic neuralgia, I have nothing good to say; it was repeatedly used by our staff, without the slightest advantage."[9]

We have come a long way in the treatment of causalgia and reflex sympathetic dystrophy, but we have no descriptions more vivid than Mitchell's of the symptoms they produce.

CASE STUDIES

Marjorie, a twenty-three-year-old domestic worker, spent an afternoon waxing floors. The next day she felt pain in the tendon at the base of her right thumb. After a few days of discomfort she consulted an orthopedic surgeon who diagnosed her problem as an inflammation of a tendon. He suggested injecting a cortisone preparation into the affected area, but Marjorie had heard bad things about cortisone and refused. The doctor then prescribed an anti-inflammatory drug and immobilized her wrist in a cast for her comfort. Marjorie went around holding her fingers completely rigid, fearful of feeling any pain at all. Within two days the wrist and hand had become hot, swollen, and excruciatingly painful, and the doctor had the cast removed. Marjorie refused to let anyone touch the area because of the increased burning pain that contact produced. The severity of the pain suggested an acute form of arthritis or possibly a deep-seated infection. Marjorie was hospitalized, and further studies failed to reveal any evidence of infection but did show distinctly that the bones of the wrist were thinning. The problem then became apparent—reflex sympathetic dystrophy. With appropriate medical and physical therapy, Marjorie's pain and swelling rapidly subsided. However, it was weeks before she could move her wrist comfortably.

Reflex sympathetic dystrophy appeared in Marjorie's case in a typical manner—following a trivial injury. It is possible, though by no means certain, that it was triggered by her fear of pain and by her keeping her fingers motionless.

Also, we know that emotional stress can accentuate the pain and discomfort of the sympathetic dystrophies once they have occurred. The question has often been raised as to whether emotional stress and a heightened sensitivity to pain, for example from an injury, play any role in causing the sympathetic dystrophies. Some authorities believe that this is the case in some but certainly not all instances. The answer has important implications for prevention, which we will discuss later.

David, a fifty-six-year-old carpenter, was admitted to a small community hospital after having fallen from a roof and sustaining severe neck pain. X rays taken of his cervical spine revealed no fracture. After three days David began complaining of pain in his left shoulder and, a day later, in his left hand. The pain had a burning quality to it and was soon associated with a swelling of the hand and an inability to move his wrist and fingers. The changing symptoms suggested undetected injuries to his left upper arm, an acute arthritis, or an infection. Further X rays and laboratory studies failed to confirm any of these possibilities, and David was transferred to a university medical center. There, specialists reconsidered all the previous possible diagnoses and added another possibility—reflex sympathetic dystrophy. Further X rays showed that within a week evidence of a remarkable amount of osteoporosis (calcium loss from the bone) had appeared in his shoulder, hand, and wrist, and David was diagnosed as having the form of reflex sympathetic dystrophy called shoulder-hand syndrome. With appropriate therapy, he eventually made a good recovery.

The confusion arising from the tendency of reflex sympathetic dystrophy to mimic arthritis and other conditions is compounded by the fact that its symptoms of pain and skin changes can occur at a bodily site distant from that of the initial and presumably precipitating injury. However, David's condition contained a diagnostic clue, for arthritis rarely produces a loss of calcium from the bones as rapid as that seen in David's shoulder, wrist, and hand. It was this relatively great loss in calcium that suggested the diagnosis of reflex sympathetic dystrophy.

THOSE AT RISK

It will be useful to summarize the myriad circumstances under which the sympathetic dystrophies occur. As noted, sometimes they appear with no apparent reason, seemingly out of the blue. This is uncommon, however, and some precipitating factor—some type of injury, inflammation, or other "insult" to the body tissues—is usually quite apparent. The injury may be severe, such as a gunshot or other penetrating wound to the tissues, or a trivial sprain to any part of an extremity. It may even be a needed surgical procedure, such as removal of a herniated disc in the lumbar area, the correction of a carpal tunnel syndrome, or abdominal surgery. A fracture in an extremity or a neck injury can also be the culprit. Such diverse disorders as gout, tendinitis, stroke, and heart attack can all be the sparks that set off the burning pain in an extremity. In short, as with several other of the soft-tissue disorders we've seen, many factors can lead to the same result—reflex sympathetic dystrophy, causalgia, and, in extreme cases, Sudeck's atrophy.

As to which medical conditions may lead to reflex sympathetic dystrophy, consider a Mayo Clinic report of one hundred forty clinic patients with this disorder. The largest single subgroup within the one hundred forty—one patient out of every four—was seen for shoulder-hand syndrome following heart attacks.[10] Tendinitis of the shoulder was the second most frequent condition seen within the group—almost one out of seven patients exhibited this condition. In regard to injuries, causalgia occurs in an estimated 2 to 5 percent of all the nerve injuries seen in major trauma centers, a far higher percentage than is seen following nontraumatic illnesses.

Youth itself used to be seen as a protection against the sympathetic dystrophies, and therefore these conditions were considered uncommon in children. We now know that this is not the case, and reports of these disorders in children are increasing, although most cases do appear in adults.

Accurate statistics in relation to sex are difficult to collect, since different medical centers deal with different patient populations and record their data in different ways. Despite the lack of documentation on this point, however, it is safe to say that the sympathetic dystrophies are no respecter of either sex.

PREVENTION

It is obvious from our survey of the various circumstances under which the sympathetic dystrophies arise that prevention is impossible in most situations. A fracture may have to be immobilized in a cast; severe pain from shoulder tendinitis may prevent any significant motion in the shoulder; injuries may be unavoidable; and so on. But experience has shown that one factor is helpful in preventing the disorders and, as we will see, is also extremely important in their treatment. That factor is the early mobilization—or movement—of an injured body part.

We have known for many years that restricting motion of any body part, no matter how necessary, has deleterious effects. If, for example, a leg is put at complete rest, it begins to exhibit adverse changes. The muscles gradually become weaker and lose substance, and since the leg muscles act as pumps to help move the blood in the veins back to the heart, the blood may pool in those veins, causing the leg to swell. The joints, deprived of motion, begin to stiffen and lose their flexibility. And the bones also suffer, for a potent stimulus to maintaining strong bones is the stress of the muscles pulling against the bones. When this pull is diminished, the bones lose calcium and become thin, or osteoporotic. Because blood flow and nutrition to the area have been altered, subtle changes also occur in the skin: The skin becomes thinner, and hair is lost on the affected area. In short, the changes that occur when motion is restricted are similar to those associated with the sympathetic dystrophies, though they occur much more slowly in the former circumstance.

Authorities on reflex sympathetic dystrophy have long stressed the importance of early mobilization in preventing the disease. In fact, the same concept is widely accepted in the treatment of many medical disorders: Movement and exercise are considered essential to the maintenance of good health and are instituted as soon as they are medically warranted. The wisdom of this principle may seem obvious, but many people accept it in word only and not in deed.

All too often, people feeling even mild pain and fatigue—and their friends and families as well—interpret these symptoms as signs that complete rest is called for. This is frequently a well meaning and sympathetic response to a person's discomfort. Unfortunately, the body might respond to inactivity and immobility with its own sympathetic answer—reflex sympathetic dystrophy or the other adverse effects described above.

We are fortunate that in these times we have available to us medications to reduce pain, but in some instances pain cannot be *completely* eradicated without such undesirable side effects as mental dullness and addiction to the medications themselves. Our goal in using pain medication must be to achieve a balance between making the discomfort tolerable and keeping the patient clearheaded enough to function. Achieving and maintaining this balance can be a delicate matter, involving our individual understanding of the situation and our ability to tolerate pain.

I am belaboring this point for a number of reasons. In an earlier chapter I pointed out that pain produces the very factors that tend to increase its intensity—irritability, tension, and depression. Furthermore, the more pain one perceives, the more one is inclined toward immobilizing the painful area—a sure route to disrupting the body's healing ability. This vicious cycle plays a large part in perpetuating the sympathetic dystrophies, but it can be broken.

TREATMENT

There are three major ingredients in any treatment program directed at curing the sympathetic dystrophies. The first is to reduce pain to a level that is tolerable and that allows motion. The second is to institute aggressive physical therapy to maintain and improve muscle, joint, and bone function. The third is to reduce the effects of the overly reactive sympathetic nervous system contributing to the pain and altered metabolism. These methods have proven to be very effective in reducing or eradicating the consequences of the sympathetic dystrophies.

Pain reduction, the first essential element, can be accomplished in many ways. If the pain is not too severe, heat or cold might reduce it. If the pain is intense, medications such as codeine or stronger narcotics may be needed, with the understanding that they should be discontinued as soon as possible. In contrast to Dr. Mitchell's experience in the Civil War, there are a few reports of the successful use of acupuncture for pain relief, but acupuncture is often ineffective and is not widely used in this country. Physical therapy is extremely important and must be undertaken as soon as the diagnosis is made. An experienced physician or physical therapist can formulate an appropriate therapeutic program, but the patient must be an active participant, making every attempt possible to move the affected muscles and joints and to allow nature to assist in the healing process. To do so may be difficult and uncomfortable, but considering the goal, it's worth the fight.

The third essential, blockading the excess effects of the sympathetic nervous system, can be accomplished in many ways. In mild cases of reflex sympathetic dystrophy, pain reduction and physical therapy alone may do the job. In more severe cases, surgical or pharmacological methods may be called on.

Here and there along the course of the sympathetic nervous system are what we might call "junction boxes," or collections of cells called ganglia. The two main ones are located near the neck and lower spine; these are called the cervical and lumbar sympathetic ganglia, respectively. It is possible to block sympathetic impulses temporarily by injecting these areas with an anesthetic agent such as lidocaine. This alone may be enough to break the sympathetic dystrophy cycle. If not, the ganglia can be removed surgically, with a more permanent effect. Modern pharmacology now offers the option of doing the same thing with medications, often avoiding the need for injections or surgery.

Many medications have been used to suppress the activity of the sympathetic nervous system and to block the effects of its adrenaline production or the inflammation that results.

Cortisone and its derivatives, such as prednisone, are often effective in this regard. Reserpine, a medication that is widely used to combat hypertension, has also been used with good results. More recently, an entirely new class of medications has been formulated that blocks the effects of adrenaline on the heart, blood vessels, and other tissues. The first of these was propranolol. A detailed description of these and the other medications used is beyond the scope of this book; it is enough to say here that rapid advances are being made in this field. Thanks to Dr. Silas Weir Mitchell and the innumerable dedicated medical investigators who followed him, the debilitating effects of the sympathetic dystrophies are yielding to efforts of modern medical science.

8

Medical Masquerades: The Imitators of Soft-Tissue Rheumatism

SCRATCHING THE SURFACE

We have made clear that differentiating one disease from another is an important part of making a diagnosis. Many medical disorders mimic and masquerade as different illnesses. We have seen this many times already; for instance, the symptoms of fibrositis may resemble those of polymyalgia rheumatica, which in turn may suggest arthritis.

The resemblances we have remarked on are superficial ones, however. When we scratch the surface of these mimics we find marked differences between them and the disorders they appear to be. So far, we have concentrated on helping you to recognize the features of an array of soft-tissue rheumatic diseases. The point has been to help you suspect which one you might have and emphasize those characteristics that distinguish it from arthritis. In short, up to now this book has functioned as a guide to what soft-tissue rheumatism *is*. Now we turn to what soft-tissue rheumatism *isn't*. The objective is to sharpen the image of the rheumatism disorders while supplying a compendium of the other possibilities that might suggest themselves along with soft-tissue rheumatism.

If I attempted to describe all the diseases and syndromes that can pose as soft-tissue rheumatism, the result would be exhausting for reader and author alike. To protect both our interests, I will concentrate on the most common arthritic diseases and other nonrheumatic imitators. Keep in mind that the presence of these disorders, and of arthritis in particular, doesn't rule out the possibility of soft-tissue rheumatic problems. Experience has shown that, if anything, the presence of such illnesses makes soft-tissue rheumatism somewhat more likely.

ARTHRITIC DISORDERS

To reiterate, the term *arthritis* refers specifically to a joint disorder and is often, but not invariably, associated with joint swelling. The list of arthritic diseases alone is a long one and includes illnesses due to trauma, degenerative changes, metabolic abnormalities, and immunologic causes. Infectious agents such as bacteria, viruses, fungi, and parasites also count among the causative agents. The different arthritic diseases have little in common with one another beyond the fact that, by definition, they affect one or more joints. We'll look at four different arthritic diseases in this section—osteoarthritis, rheumatoid arthritis, gout, and gonorrhea—paying special attention to the features that can cause them to be confused with one or more of the soft-tissue rheumatic diseases.

OSTEOARTHRITIS

Osteoarthritis is also called "degenerative" arthritis. This name reflects the belief, now in contention, that the illness is primarily degenerative rather than inflammatory in nature. The degeneration was considered to be due to a breakdown of the cartilage in the joints from aging or such abnormal factors as faulty metabolism or poor nutrition. Evidence now suggests that inflammation often plays a significant role, so the term osteoarthritis seems less restrictive and more appropriate.

Osteoarthritis can affect any joint containing articular cartilage. Most commonly, the fingers, knees, hips, and spine are involved. Early osteoarthritis does not always show up in X rays. Pain is a prominent feature, but it is not uncommon for marked X-ray findings of osteoarthritis to be associated with little or no pain at all.

In diagnosis, the proximity of areas of osteoarthritis to joint capsules, ligaments, and tendons can make it a little tricky to distinguish osteoarthritis from soft-tissue rheumatism. One area where diagnosis can be particularly ambiguous is the base of the thumb, where the common tendon inflammation called De Quervain's tenosynovitis can easily be interpreted as osteoarthritis, especially by the sufferers themselves. But knowing some anatomy and being able to literally put your finger on the source of the pain will help you determine whether a tendon (soft-tissue rheumatism) or joint (arthritis) is involved, though a doctor's participation is necessary for true diagnosis and treatment.

In a turnabout of the usual diagnostic confusion, osteoarthritis is often mistaken for bursitis of the shoulder. A small joint called the acromioclavicular joint—where the clavicle, or "collar bone," meets a projection on the scapula (the shoulder blade) called the acromion process—lies in close proximity to the capsules and tendons of the shoulder joint. When the acromioclavicular joint is affected by osteoarthritis, considerable pain results when the shoulder is moved. The condition often responds to an injection of a cortisone medication into the joint, but if the injection is directed toward the usual bursitis or tendinitis areas in the erroneous belief that the problem is with the soft tissues, the patient will experience no relief at all.

The knee is a Pandora's box of problems, with its many cartilages, ligaments, tendons, and bursas. A torn cartilage or a small area of osteoarthritis on the inside of the knee can be difficult to distinguish from an inflamed ligament. At times, making a conclusive diagnosis involves more than feeling around and getting plain X rays to pinpoint the difficulty. The examining doctor might need to make arthrograms (X rays taken after a radio-opaque dye is injected into the knee) or to view the inside of the joint through an arthroscope. As we have already discussed, sometimes a swelling involving the bursas appears behind the knee. This is called a Baker's, or popliteal, cyst, and the underlying cause is not soft-tissue rheumatism but a problem within the knee joint itself.

Osteoarthritis of the hip joint usually causes pain within that joint itself that seems to come from deep within the groin. The pain can be referred to the knee, and I often see patients with hip arthritis who complain only of knee pain. The pain of trochanteric bursitis, however, is on the outer side of the hip and often makes it difficult to lie on the affected side. This difference in the pain site helps to distinguish the bursitis from arthritis of the hip. A test to indicate possible hip joint problems is to lie on your back, pull one knee to your chest, and move the knee to the side. If this movement is painful or restricted, the problem may be in the hip. I say *may be* because a tendinitis in the inner part of the thigh can give the same symptoms.

Osteoarthritis of the spine, also known as osteoarthrosis, can be painful though surprisingly it occurs without symptoms in many people. A spine can appear amazingly arthritic on an X ray and still cause the patient no pain whatever. If you have an arthritic spine, it is possible that some or all of your discomfort may be due to ligament or muscle tension problems. A protrusion of a disc (known as a herniated disc) in the cervical or lumbar spine areas can cause pain due to pressure on nerve roots. Since the fibrous discs—the strong fibrous connective tissue between the vertebrae—do not show up on X rays, special tests such as CAT scans (computerized axial tomography) or myelograms (X rays taken after radio-opaque dye is injected into the spinal canal) may be needed to show the problem.

Rheumatoid Arthritis

Rheumatoid arthritis is an inflammatory disease of unknown cause. The tissue's reaction to injury, which we call *inflam-*

mation, involves the calling forth of white blood cells and other complex bodily defense mechanisms. The results are varying degrees of the classical signs of inflammation noted often in this book—pain, swelling, warmth, and redness of the skin. The hallmark of rheumatoid arthritis is joint swelling; where this symptom is not present one cannot make a definite diagnosis of rheumatoid arthritis. The American Rheumatism Association has published some fairly rigid guidelines to help physicians decide if rheumatoid arthritis is present. Depending on the signs and symptoms, the diagnosis may be possible, probable, definite, or classical rheumatoid arthritis.

Rheumatoid arthritis can affect other tissues besides the joints. The marked muscle stiffness it can cause mimics that in fibrositis and polymyalgia rheumatica. If joint swelling is present but undetected, it is easy to see how the two can be confused. In fact, as I mentioned earlier, joint swelling has been noted in some cases of polymyalgia rheumatica, raising some questions as to whether or not the criteria used for diagnosing rheumatoid arthritis should be revised. Usually the situation is quite clear, but at times distinguishing between the two diseases is extremely difficult.

If you have rheumatoid arthritis, it's important *not* to attribute every one of your aches and pains to it. Rheumatoid arthritis in no way makes you immune to the more easily treated conditions such as tennis elbow, trochanteric bursitis, and the like. Tendinitis occurs frequently with rheumatoid arthritis and can be a part of the rheumatoid process. In such a case, the tendinitis is surprisingly less painful than those types described earlier.

Another condition that frequently accompanies rheumatoid arthritis is carpal tunnel syndrome. Where this condition is present, the pain, tingling, or numbness that occurs in the hand is *not* joint pain and can be relieved in almost all cases—if recognized for what it is and appropriately treated.

Gout

Gout is an acute inflammatory arthritis of metabolic origin that occurs when uric acid, one of the body's waste products, crystallizes in a joint. The result is a very painful, swollen, and red joint. Gout often occurs in the bunion joint of the big toe, but it can affect other toes, the ankles, knees, or other joints in the arms and legs. Gout hardly ever affects the hips, shoulder, or spine, despite what you may have read or believe. It can mimic reflex sympathetic dystrophy, but as I said before, the problem is usually the other way around—reflex sympathetic dystrophy is more likely to be thought of as gout (or some other disease).

What is *not* as well known is that gout can affect tendons and particularly the Achilles tendon, which attaches to the heel. Gout at this site is easily confused with non-gouty Achilles' tendinitis.

Gonorrhea

As we have said, gonorrhea is a venereal disease caused by the bacteria known as the gonococcus. The usual manifestations that most people are aware of are a urethral discharge in men and pelvic inflammatory disease in women. Gonorrhea is more complex and treacherous than that, however. It is not widely appreciated that some men and women carry the gonococcus bacteria for months without any symptoms at all. The first symptom may be an acute and painful arthritis or a tendinitis.

The tendinitis associated with gonorrhea often has two unusual aspects that help differentiate it from the tendinitis of soft-tissue rheumatism: The inflammation may migrate from one tendon to another, and a fever is often present. Another clue that is sometimes present is shaking chills. I have never seen a case of tendinitis from a noninfectious cause that was associated with shaking chills.

As I mentioned earlier, gonorrhea is not the only bacteria that can cause tendinitis, but it is one of the more common ones, particularly in young sexually active men and women.

HORMONAL ABNORMALITIES

A hormone is a compound produced in an organ or gland and secreted into the bloodstream. Hormones are carried to other organs and tissues and stimulate their activity.

I have often been asked by patients who have a rheumatic disease whether a "hormone deficiency" might be the cause. The answer is sometimes yes but most often no. It's beyond the scope of this book to detail all the possible problems that can result from hormone imbalances, but some may lead you to think you have a soft-tissue rheumatic problem. The one most likely to do so is a thyroid hormone deficiency. Let's turn to a detailed look at thyroid problems and a more cursory view of some other hormone problems and their association (or lack of association) with soft-tissue rheumatism.

Thyroid Hormone Abnormalities

The thyroid gland lies in front of the trachea, just beneath the notch at the upper end of the sternum, or breastbone. This gland has a right and left lobe connected by what is called an isthmus. The hormone that this gland produces, the thyroid hormone, is essential to normal body metabolism. Simply put, an excess speeds up metabolism and a deficiency slows it down. We'll consider excess production first.

The effects of too much thyroid hormone are collectively called *hyperthyroidism*. The early total picture is one of hyperactivity of the body. Muscle activity increases, often to the point of muscle tremors. The body burns more calories, and weight loss frequently occurs, even when food intake increases. The pulse rate accelerates, the blood pressure rises, and an intolerance to heat appears. In short, hyperthyroidism can drive the body to the point of total exhaustion. This condition is rarely confused with soft-tissue rheumatism, but the story is different when there is a deficiency of thyroid hormone.

John, a thirty-six-year-old carpenter, had always been in good health. He had a particular interest in body building and had outfitted his garage with weights and gadgets to help him develop his muscles. Over the course of six months he noticed a gradual aching and stiffness in his muscles. He tried taking aspirin, but it didn't help. He felt stiff all day and just couldn't seem to loosen his muscles. The more weight lifting he did, the worse he got. He found that he was getting weaker instead of stronger. His appetite was poor, but he didn't lose weight—a fact he attributed to his decreased activity. He was under a considerable amount of stress in his marriage, and the economic climate had resulted in less work for him and a decreased income. He felt depressed and was certain that this was part of his problem. John's doctor thought he had fibrositis. Just to be sure that nothing else was wrong, however, the doctor ordered a battery of blood tests, including one to measure thyroid hormone level. When the tests came back, the answer was there. John had a very low level of thyroid hormone in his blood. Treatment was begun with a thyroid hormone, and John's "fibrositis" gradually disappeared.

A thyroid hormone deficiency causes the symptoms that are collectively known as *hypothyroidism*. In this condition the function of many body organs and tissues goes into slow motion, with widespread and adverse effects. The symptoms depend partly on how much thyroid hormone is present and partly on which organ or tissue is affected the most. The muscles are very sensitive to the lack of thyroid hormone and respond with aching, stiffness, and eventual weakness. It is easy to see how these symptoms can be interpreted as either fibrositis or polymyalgia rheumatica. A telltale difference, however, is that in hypothyroidism exercising the muscles doesn't seem to loosen them up. It often makes the situation worse. This is not a hard-and-fast rule, but it can be helpful. The other effects of hypothyroidism can include a deepened and husky voice, cold intolerance, weight gain, congestive heart failure, swelling of the skin, and mental dullness. If the thyroid hormone deficiency is severe, a psychotic state can ensue, and the condition can even be fatal. The treatment is simplicity itself: a daily oral dose of a thyroid hormone.

Calcium Metabolism and the Parathyroid Glands

The parathyroid glands, which lie beneath the thyroid gland, produce a substance called the parathyroid hormone. This hormone affects calcium metabolism and is essential for the maintenance of good bone structure. If the glands produce too much parathyroid hormone, the level of serum calcium rises and calcium is extracted from the bones, which causes them to become "osteoporotic" and more easily fractured. This condition is most readily detected by obtaining a serum calcium level and getting X rays of the bones, but a new technique, bone densitometry, is more accurate in confirming osteoporosis. Osteoporosis can occur even if normal levels of parathyroid hormones are present. This disease is most often seen in postmenopausal women.

The osteoporosis frequently seen in postmenopausal women can be the cause of pain in the spine and fractures. It is not usually accompanied by a parathyroid hormone excess and is partly due to a decreased calcium intake, but also to lack of the female hormone called estrogen, discussed below.

If the parathyroid glands don't produce enough hormone, then the calcium level in the blood is low; if it gets low enough, muscle cramps can result. In general, symptoms do not occur unless the levels of the parathyroid hormone are extremely high or low. Muscle cramps, for example, are very common in perfectly healthy people and are rarely due to low blood calcium or a calcium deficiency.

There are many consequences of a disordered calcium metabolism, but the only significant symptom that can be confused with the soft-tissue rheumatic diseases is pain in the spinal area.

Cortisone and the Adrenal Cortex

Adrenocortical hormones are produced by the outer layer (the cortex) of the adrenal glands. These glands lie adjacent to and just above the kidneys. They produce the "cortisone" group of hormones that are important in maintaining many tissues and body responses. (Cortisone and its derivatives have been synthesized by biochemists and used to treat many rheumatic diseases.) These hormones affect sodium and potassium metabolism, muscle function, and skin and other organs, and are important in our responses to stress and infection.

A deficiency of the adrenocortical hormones results in weakness, weight loss, low blood pressure, and an *increased* serum potassium, and other deleterious consequences collectively known as "Addison's disease." If the adrenal gland overproduces the cortisone hormones, the result is *loss* of body potassium, high blood pressure, weight gain, osteoporosis, thinning of the skin, and a host of other abnormalities collectively known as "Cushing's syndrome." A lack of or an excess of adrenal hormones may cause vague muscle and bone aching that is easily confused with a rheumatic disease.

Estrogens and Testosterone

Estrogens and testosterone are the "sex" hormones. They determine the female and male characteristics respectively. The estrogens are produced in the ovaries, and testosterone is made in the testes. We can dispense with any further discussion of testosterone, since the symptoms of too little or too much are unlikely to be confused with soft-tissue rheumatism.

Estrogen production decreases markedly with menopause, a common symptom of which are hot flashes. Are musculoskeletal aches and pains in postmenopausal women caused by estrogen deficiency, or should we be alerted to the possibility of soft-tissue rheumatism when they appear in this group? By way of answering this question, let's consider what effects the estrogens have on the muscles, connective tissues, and bones.

The estrogens are not known to play any significant role in the functioning of the muscles and connective tissues. They do have an important role in the calcium metabolism in bone, however. Women begin to lose small amounts of calcium from their bones prior to menopause—in some cases as early as ten to twenty years before estrogen production ceases. The process accelerates after menopause, and some women develop severe calcium losses and their bones become more fracturable. This condition is known as postmenopausal osteoporosis. Extensive loss of calcium in the spine can lead to spontaneous fractures of the vertebrae, resulting in pain and loss of height. The pain can be anywhere in the back and almost always extends to the muscles surrounding the spine.

The pain and stiffness of postmenopausal osteoporosis can resemble that of polymyalgia rheumatica, but there are some differences. In polymyalgia rheumatica the discomfort is primarily in the hip, shoulder, and neck areas, while in osteoporosis it is mainly in the spinal area. Usually, osteoporosis presents no great diagnostic problem, unless both conditions are present at the same time.

Treating this type of osteoporosis means supplying the body with what it needs in order to improve the deposition of calcium in the bones. There are two, and perhaps three, mainstays of therapy. The first is to increase the intake of calcium, average supplements being from 1,000 to 1,500 milligrams (1.0 to 1.5 grams). A word of caution is necessary here: The numbers refer to the amount of *calcium* in the supplement. Calcium supplements come from different sources, such as oyster shells and dolomite (a calcium and magnesium supplement). If the label on the bottle says, "Each tablet contains 250 milligrams of calcium carbonate," only 40 percent of each tablet, or 100 milligrams, is calcium; the rest is carbonate. Ten such tablets would be required to give 1,000 milligrams of calcium. Some nonprescription calcium supplements contain 500 milligrams of *calcium* in each tablet, so only two are needed to give 1,000 milligrams.

The second mainstay of treatment is estrogen replacement therapy. The appropriateness of this treatment must be determined on an individual basis, since there are some possible side effects.

The third treatment frequently used for estrogen deficiency is vitamin D. When the body is exposed to sunlight, it is capable of synthesizing vitamin D, and supplements may or may not be needed. As with all the therapies, a doctor should make this decision.

But what about our original question: Does estrogen deficiency cause diffuse aches and pains in the postmenopausal woman? In general, I don't believe that it does, and I haven't read anything to make me think otherwise. Therefore, where musculoskeletal pains are a problem in women of this age group, soft-tissue rheumatic disorders should be considered possible explanations.

Potassium Deficiency

Many minerals are essential to maintaining health, and mineral deficiencies have a vast number of possible effects. In the context of the soft-tissue rheumatic diseases, the mineral deficiency of concern is potassium deficiency. This condition is a common cause of muscle dysfunction. A higher concentration of potassium is found in the muscles than in the blood. If the body has a potassium deficiency, muscle cramps and weakness result. The weakness *per se* is not associated with aches and pains, and that helps distinguish it from soft-tissue rheumatism. If much cramping is present, the symptoms superficially can suggest fibrositis or polymyalgia rheumatica, but the cramping caused by a potassium deficiency occurs in the arms and legs rather than the shoulder and hip areas, as in the latter disorders.

Potassium deficiencies can result from many causes but are rarely found in people who are not on diuretics, or so-called water pills. Diuretics—such as the thiazide group or chlorthalidone—are prescribed for such disorders as high blood pressure and fluid accumulation, which itself can stem from a variety of causes. These medications are notorious for causing not only the desired effect of urinary sodium loss but also considerable potassium loss. I might add that other types of diuretics, such as spironolactone and triamterine, can cause potassium *retention,* so it is important to know which diuretic you are taking. In any event, if the urinary potassium loss exceeds the potassium intake, the result can be severe muscle weakness. In this case, the symptom signals not a rheumatic disease but a mineral deficiency that needs prompt correction.

INFECTIONS AND INFESTATIONS

Weakness, fatigue, and musculoskeletal aches and pain are symptoms of soft-tissue rheumatism, but they can also be subtle signs of an underlying infection or infestation. The term *infection* means the invasion of the body by a microorganism such as a bacteria, virus, or fungus, with the subsequent production of inflammation and its consequences. *Infestation* means the harboring in the body of a parasite. The presence of a fever strongly suggests, but is not diagnostic of, an infection.

Polymyalgia rheumatica, giant cell arteritis, and the tendinitis caused by infection can all be accompanied by a fever. It is very helpful to have a thermometer in the house to ascertain whether a fever is actually present. That sounds obvious but, surprisingly, many people do not own one. People often believe that they can always tell if they have a fever—and they are often wrong. I frequently see people in my office who say they have no fever with their illness, only to find that their temperature is 100 degrees or higher during their visit.

What exactly is a fever, then? We tend to think of an oral temperature of 98.6 degrees Fahrenheit as "normal," but there is considerable variation in healthy individuals; the normal range is generally considered to be 96.5 to 99.0 degrees when the temperature is taken while the person is at rest or after only moderate activity. The lowest body temperature in a normal individual occurs about two to four o'clock in the morning, and the temperature often rises slowly to a peak in the late afternoon or evening. Rectal temperatures can be up to one degree higher than oral readings. A very hot bath, a lot of exercise, or something hot in the mouth can cause a brief rise in a normal temperature.

As for muscle aches and pains specifically, they can signal soft-tissue rheumatism but they also accompany many hard-to-diagnose illnesses, such as bacterial endocarditis, viral hepatitis, and kidney infections, and can be present for a long time before more specific symptoms of these nonrheumatic illnesses appear. Thus a rheumatic illness might be considered a possibility before the real diagnosis manifests itself. As noted earlier, shaking chills are an important clue to the possibility that your aches are due not to soft-tissue rheumatism but rather to some infection.

Parasitic infestations are very common in undeveloped countries but are seen less frequently in the United States. However, one parasitic disease occurs in this country more often than most people realize, and it can cause unexplained musculoskeletal pains. This disease is called *trichinosis,* and it is caused by eating insufficiently cooked pork that is infested with the parasite *Trichinella spiralis.* Again, a fever occurs at some time during the illness, but if the infestation is not large, a low-grade fever may go unnoticed. Once more, here is a case of a specific nonrheumatic disorder that in certain circumstances can mimic the symptoms of soft-tissue rheumatism and therefore go unrecognized—and untreated—for what it is.

PARKINSON'S DISEASE

When Parkinson's disease is fully developed, it is rarely mistaken for anything else. The sufferer has a shuffling gait, a bent posture, stiffness and slowness of motion, tremors of the hands, and an expressionless face. This disease makes its appearance in middle and late age, and usually poses no diagnostic problem. In its early stages, however, it can be subtle enough to lead you to think in terms of muscular rheumatism.

Parkinson's disease is caused by poorly understood degenerative changes in specific cells in the brain stem. The earliest symptoms may be stiffness and an overall slowdown of muscle function, with the other diagnostic features of the illness appearing only later. There is no muscle pain associated with Parkinson's disease, and it is not commonly confused with "rheumatism" unless the affected person has had a previous problem with musculoskeletal pains. Where that is the case, it is easy enough to pass off the stiffness as being due to rheumatism. Many effective treatments are available for Parkinson's disease, and early diagnosis and treatment can significantly improve general mobility.

MEDICATIONS

Modern medicine has given us a wealth of drugs to treat the illnesses that plague us. But these drugs are sometimes double-edged swords, for they can have adverse side effects that often go unrecognized. Let me mention just a few to illustrate the role they can play in musculoskeletal complaints.

I have already explained the muscle weakness and cramps that can occur from a potassium deficiency following the use of many diuretics, commonly known as "water pills." Some diuretics, particularly those in the thiazide group, can cause muscle aching and cramps before any appreciable potassium is lost. The aching is usually in the legs but can occur in ot muscles as well.

Some drugs can mimic a rheumatic disease known as systemic lupus erythematosus (SLE). SLE is a disease with many manifestations—skin lesions, arthritis, nervous system abnormalities, and muscle and joint pain, to name a few. Two commonly used medications can cause reactions indistinguishable from that of SLE. One is procainamide, a drug used to treat irregular heart rhythms, and the other is hydralazine, which is used in the treatment of hypertension.

Few people would consider vitamin A a medicine or drug, and many take large doses of this substance in the belief that it will help to prevent one disease or another. Daily doses of vitamin A in amounts over 75,000 units can cause some nasty problems, one of which is pain in the bones easily misinterpreted as some type of rheumatism.

As you know, musculoskeletal aches and pains can point to soft-tissue rheumatism as well as myriad other medical problems. It's important to stress, too, that muscular weakness or stiffness *in the absence of any aches or pains* suggests that soft-tissue rheumatism is *not* the cause. If you're having musculoskeletal problems, take a minute to think about whether you are taking any kind of medication or large doses of vitamins. It is the rare drug that is completely free of potential adverse side effects—effects that are too often forgotten when things go awry.

Arthritic and bone diseases can mimic soft-tissue rheumatism and vice versa. Keep in mind, however, that even if you have arthritis, you are not immune to any of the soft-tissue rheumatic problems. But if you have musculoskeletal problems, simply being aware of these facts and of the other clues discussed in this chapter will keep you alert to the meaning of your symptoms and perhaps help you and your doctor pinpoint the source of your illness.

9

Helping Yourself: Prevention and Treatment

A BEGINNING POINT

In the previous chapters I defined and described soft-tissue rheumatism. It should be clear by now that some types can be prevented and others cannot. However, *all* soft-tissue rheumatic disorders can be treated, often very effectively. We will now concentrate on measures you can take yourself to treat musculoskeletal pain and, where possible, to prevent it from developing. In this vein, it will be useful to review some of the important concepts touched upon in earlier chapters.

Often at social gatherings someone will mention a pain he's been feeling in some area of his musculoskeletal system, and ask, "What can you do for arthritis?" As stated, the question rests on two erroneous assumptions. The first is that the pain stems from arthritis. As you know by now, the odds are about one in three that the pain originates in soft-tissue rheumatism rather than arthritis. The second error lies in assuming that arthritis is a single entity; like soft-tissue rheumatism, it is a cluster of conditions, each with its own characteristics. Clearly, the important beginning point in discussing prevention or treatment is having the *correct diagnosis* when trouble appears and knowing the possible options that the diagnosis suggests.

It is reasonable to take some precautions to prevent tendinitis and fibrositis, for example, but unreasonable to hope to prevent polymyalgia rheumatica. If you have polymyalgia rheumatica and treat it as fibrositis, you will not get much relief. The same holds true if you have a tendinitis of the finger and treat it as arthritis. These disorders differ from each other and must be approached differently. What helps one may have no appreciable effect on the other.

No matter which soft-tissue rheumatic disorder you might have, a clear understanding of which self-help techniques are appropriate and which are not will guide you through the maze of therapies that have been tried and proved effective, sometimes over many centuries. Thus, in gaining control over your situation by clarifying it, you won't simply be a recipient of therapy; you'll be an active participant. Treatment for two disorders in particular, fibrositis and psychogenic rheumatism, depends for its effectiveness on your full understanding. Preceding chapters contained brief descriptions of effective therapies. Here I cover in more detail what you can do for yourself, and later I will go into the medical treatments available.

Some treatment methods discussed here are also valuable as preventive measures—things you can do to keep aches and pains from developing. You will see as we go on that prevention and treatment often go hand in hand. How much better it is to apply some commonsense measures to keep your muscles and tendons healthy than to wait until discomfort appears. Whether you consider the old adage to be trite and true or tried and true, an ounce of prevention is indeed worth a pound of cure.

DEALING WITH STRESS

If you laid end to end all those who are experts in dealing with emotional stress, they still wouldn't reach a conclusion. Being a rheumatologist and not an expert in stress, I'm not going to reach any conclusions either. Still, in my practice I have seen a great many people handle stress successfully, and in a discussion of prevention and self-treatment these observations have special relevance. Let me point out that my views on this matter relate to a particular sample of people: those whose stress had resulted in soft-tissue rheumatic problems such as muscle tension pains, fibrositis, and psychogenic rheumatism.

Let's start at the beginning by reviewing the notion of *emotional stress.* Stress generates internal energy that has to find an outlet somewhere. It may result in a "debit" situation—high blood pressure, an accelerated heartbeat, an irritable bowel, a duodenal ulcer—or muscle aches and pains that by their very presence create anxieties, tensions, and more stress.

Stress isn't always a negative force, however. Even for those who suffer it, stress can be downright beneficial. The energy it generates need not necessarily translate into anxieties and more stress. It can also be expressed in productive activities—advantageous both to the individual and society as a whole. Consider the results of a survey taken in 1983 by the Chemical Bank of New York. The bank questioned 1,047 small-business owners about their work lives and included questions on stress and its effects.[1] Forty-three percent of the respondents answered that they were under a moderate amount, and 37 percent under a great deal of stress. When asked about the effects of stress, 22 percent—one out of five—considered it beneficial; 43 percent, detrimental. The rest believed stress had no significant effect on them one way or the other. Those who considered stress beneficial said it made day-to-day life more interesting, increased their productivity, and helped them manage their time. Those who regarded it as detrimental claimed it caused irritability, health problems, insomnia, difficulties at home, and reduced productivity at work. Given this spread of responses, it is not unreasonable to assume that many people in all walks of life—secretarial work, housework, the creative arts, sports, you name it—are able to turn the potential problem of stress into an asset.

But in practical terms, when stress results in soft-tissue rheumatic aches and pains, how can we turn the "debit" into an "asset"? The first step is acknowledgment. If you don't recognize stress as a problem, clearly there's nothing to discuss. But if you do see stress as playing an adverse role in your life, the next necessary step is to accept the reality of the stress/pent-up internal energy/muscle aches and pain cycle. That done, you are in a position to deal with stress as many others have—very successfully.

My first true personal appreciation of "stress" stemmed from experiences during my medical internship in Philadelphia. As interns we were "on call" every other night and often worked thirty-six hours at a stretch. We had considerable responsibilities, but except for being on our feet a great deal there were no great physical demands. The fatigue that we experienced was due more to mental stress than anything else. After a few months I began to feel some muscle aches and pains that were quite new to me. Even a good night's sleep didn't help much. One evening I had the unpleasant task of telling a man that his much beloved wife had terminal cancer. Afterwards, when I sat down to dinner, I felt as though I had been run over by a truck. My first inclination was to get some sleep, but I suspected my aches weren't going to be helped that way. I put on some tennis shoes and jogged a few miles and tried to do as little thinking as possible. Then I stopped in at a club that catered to local boxers, bookies, and other businessmen. The place had a reputation for hot steam baths, an ice-cold pool, good pastrami sandwiches, and the least expensive massage in town. I partook of it all. When I left the club I felt relaxed, pain-free and, in one word, rejuvenated. I had found the "cure" for me and took it whenever time and finances permitted.

Here's another case—of Frieda, a forty-five-year-old housewife. Her husband was a successful executive who had to travel frequently. After both of their children graduated college and left home, she felt a sudden loneliness, depression, and lack of purpose in life. By her own admission much of it was the "empty nest" syndrome coupled with the fact that she had never had the time to develop her own talents. On top of it all, she developed the muscle aches, pains, and stiffness of fibrositis. She realized that she was under emotional stress, but she couldn't consider doing anything for herself because of her discomfort and fatigue. When she finally understood the dynamics of her problem, she forced herself to take some business courses and then opened a catering service with a friend. She had exchanged one stress for another, but the difference was she *enjoyed* the new stress—she was exhilarated by it. Needless to say, her symptoms of fibrositis disappeared.

Then there was Margie, who worked as a secretary in a federal prison noted for its history of violence among the prisoners. When she went to work she passed through many gates with armed guards. Margie was constantly afraid of being physically attacked. She began complaining to her physician and to whomever else would listen about severe muscle aches and pains. Suddenly one day she got the picture. She quit her job, found employment with a plumbing firm, and was simply cured, once and for all, of her "rheumatism."

Jim was president of a small firm that imported goods from Asia. He did a lot of traveling and attended many stressful business lunches lasting hours at a time. He developed neck and backaches and some very severe tension headaches. His preferred method of treatment was to increase his intake of Scotch and add some aspirin and codeine. As time passed, Jim realized the truth: He was an alcoholic. This frightening fact became a sobering one. He abruptly stopped drinking and began to turn his energies to remodeling his house—or, as he put it, "building something to last and getting rid of the booze and drugs." Much to his delight he also rid himself of his muscle pains and headaches.

Patients who have successfully dealt with stress resulting in muscle aches and pains have inevitably followed one or both of two courses. The first was simply to get out of the "debit" type of stressful situation if possible. By getting out I mean they either learned how to deal with the situation or avoided it completely. They improved even if they moved to a more stressful situation, as long as it was one they considered an "asset." At times, though, this first course of action is impossible; for any number of reasons the "debit" situation cannot be changed. I couldn't leave my internship, for instance, without the unacceptable alternative of ending my medical career. The course in that case is to release the valve on the pressure cooker and find outlets for the pent-up energy through rest, relaxation, and exercise. In every successful case I've seen, the course the people chose was one that they felt comfortable about. The lesson is familiar to you by now: The solution must come from within, not without.

SOFT TISSUES AND COMMON SENSE

Our muscles, tendons, ligaments, and the like are subject to the wear and tear of daily living. The terms wear and tear, although certainly not original with Dr. Silas Weir Mitchell, were well defined by him more than a hundred years ago:

> *Wear* is a natural and legitimate result of lawful use and is what we all have to put up with as a result of years of activity of brain and body. *Tear* is another matter: It comes of hard or evil usage of body or engine, of putting things to wrong purposes, using a chisel for a screwdriver, a penknife for a gimlet. Long strain, or the sudden demand of strength from weakness, causes tear. Wear comes of use; tear of abuse.[2]

Dr. Mitchell's words are particularly applicable to our soft tissues. Although admirably designed, they are easily damaged by the stresses and strains we subject them to. Wear is inevitable, but tear is often avoidable. "Long strain, or the sudden demand of strength from weakness" is often the starting point of soft tissue aches and pains. Our muscles and other soft tissues serve us best when we are aware of their needs.

PREVENTIVE MAINTENANCE I: REST VERSUS RELAXATION

If the stresses one experiences are so constant that the muscles have no time to rest, relax, and recuperate, the aches and pains themselves become a source of anxiety and stress, which sets in motion a vicious cycle of discomfort and misery. This is one "long strain" that we can prevent, often by interrupting the destructive cycle. The key is to provide our muscles time for rest and relaxation, allowing a period of repair and rejuvenation.

Recall that *rest* and *relaxation* are not synonymous. Rest is freedom from activity; relaxation is recreation and diversion that refreshes our strength. Too often people mistakenly think they are doing one or the other or both when what they are really doing is perpetuating the tension-pain cycle. The result, of course, is that "they just don't seem to help at all."

Picture a hypothetical situation: You're on vacation and basking in the sun on a beautiful Hawaiian beach. The palm trees are gently swaying in a warm tropical breeze, and the air is filled with the fragrance of exotic plants and the salty air from the ocean. Your mind is filled with thoughts: How much the trip is costing you, whether you cancelled the newspaper, what your kids are up to back home, and your susceptibility to a sunburn. You are resting but you aren't relaxing—and you're getting a little edgy and achy. Just as you told your doctor, even resting doesn't do a bit of good for your pains. It's time for the tennis game and for some diversion and relaxation. Tennis is great—it's a chance for a little competition. You've taken lessons at the club and worked your way up the ladder. The problem is that your spouse is not as good as you are, and doubles are a pain in the neck, since you usually lose. That's why you prefer singles—you have a better chance to win. You're still tense and aching during the game, and indeed you do lose the game that day. "Damn it," you mutter to yourself, "I could have relaxed as much at home and saved a few grand."

Resting is necessary to restore our energies. But if our minds are not relaxed at these times, resting becomes just one more opportunity to rehash our worries and generate more tension to feed our aches and pains. If rest gives you no relief from discomfort, it may well be that anxieties, fears, hostilities, competitiveness, and unresolved conflicts are preventing true rest. In the same way, inner turmoil could be defeating your attempts at relaxation—turning recreation and diversion into just another source of muscle aches and pains rather than the refreshment you need.

Many of us expect medications to "cure" the life problems that inhibit our rest and relaxation. But the potent analgesic and anti-inflammatory medications available yield only temporary relief at best when marital, sexual, or financial concerns are undermining our attempts to relax.

Each of us must choose the methods that work best for us individually, be it a walk in the woods, a bicycle ride, a humorous movie, a noncompetitive sport, a good book, meditation, conversations with friends—any type of pleasant, *guilt-free* diversion that temporarily frees our mind from its burdens. I stress *guilt-free* particularly for those who are fastidious, perfectionistic, and compulsive. You must choose something you enjoy and can do in a fully relaxed manner. A bit of hedonism can be very good for you—certainly more effective and safer than lots of aspirin. Remember, only you can prevent the "long strain."

PREVENTIVE MAINTENANCE II: EXERCISE—YOUR CHOICE

Not only the long strain but "the sudden demand of strength from weakness" can have deleterious effects on our soft tissues. As I noted earlier, every material on earth has its breaking point. Soft tissues, being what they are, are certainly no exception. Misuse results in muscle strains, inflammations such as tendinitis and ligamentitis, and even tears and ruptures of tissues. No matter how well meant is the misuse and abuse, the soft tissues remain unforgiving. It's estimated that in the United States our population suffers more than 100 million days of restricted activity and more than 24 million days of disability yearly requiring bed rest—from sprains and strains alone![3] With some preventive maintenance, much pain and misery can be avoided.

You might ask, "How much exercise is needed and what kind?" The answer lies in another question: "What are your goals?" Body building, heart-attack prevention, weight loss, preparation for skiing, or perhaps the avoidance of muscle aches and pains from just the daily stresses of everyday life? Our concern here is the latter—avoiding common, everyday forms of muscle abuse. Let's consider a few garden-variety forms of soft-tissue abuse and the kinds of exercise that prevent them.

Jane is a stockbroker and just about wedded to her telephone. For many hours each day that instrument is tucked against her ear and supported by her shoulder. Furthermore, whenever she goes out she carries a handbag slung over her shoulder that is filled with essentials and weighs about eight pounds. By evening Jane has her usual headache and pains across the back of her shoulders. Now consider Dan, a computer programmer who sits every day in a poorly designed chair and types for hours. His day ends with low back and neck aches. What these two have in common is that they maintain certain muscles in one position and under stress for long periods of time. The prevention is simple: a program of frequent breaks and muscle stretches.

It's spring-cleaning time, and Stephanie's going at it with a vengeance. She scrubs the floors, walls, and everything else she can get her hands on. Her reward? A clean house and a very painful "tennis elbow." Merv jogs two miles a day. There's an eight-mile race to celebrate Groundhog Day, and he enters it. He comes in third. His reward? A bronze medal and one devil of an Achilles' tendinitis.

The common denominator here is the sudden demand of strength from weakness—the pull of muscles on tendons and tendon attachments unaccustomed and unconditioned to persistent strain. Prevention is possible by the simple expedient of intermittent rather than prolonged activity, and the gradual conditioning of muscles and tendons.

These lessons in exercise use are simple but effective. First, avoid prolonged contraction of muscles. Intermittent muscle relaxation and stretching are both preventive and therapeutic. Second, don't demand strength from weakness. Pace and prepare yourself. If you don't, your soft tissues will reprimand you with stiffness, aches, and pains.

And remember, of course, when deciding how you'll approach your problem, that the proper exercises for you are not only the ones you need for your purposes but the ones you enjoy. If you don't enjoy them, chances are you won't do them for long.

There is no shortage of advice on exercising. In preparing this chapter I did a computer search of books in print related to physical exercise and found a grand total of 348. Add to this radio and television shows on exercise, advice and guidance in magazines and newspapers, advice from professionals and nonprofessionals alike, and you come up with a staggering and bewildering collection. It's your choice, so pick those that meet your goals and suit your character, and then stick with the program. You have nothing to lose but your aches and pains.

CHANGING THE TEMPERATURE

Temperature change is a time-honored approach to the temporary relief of muscle and other soft-tissue aches and pains. Both heat and cold can work but under different circumstances.

HEAT

The local application of heat to the skin will cause increased blood flow due to dilatation, or widening, of blood vessels. If the heat penetrates to the muscles, the same effect occurs there, and with increased blood flow comes improved muscle nutrition and relaxation. Aches, pains, and stiffness may all recede under heat. However, if the discomfort is caused by acute inflammation, such as an active tendinitis or that following a ligament sprain, the result could well be more rather than less pain. The reason is that the increased blood flow causes more swelling of the tissues and brings in more white blood cells to participate in the inflammatory response. You may have had this experience with a fresh ankle sprain, an active tennis elbow, or bursitis of the shoulder, as examples. Heat is generally most effective, therefore, in the latter stages of inflammation, as in chronic bursitis and tendinitis, or when there is little or no acute inflammation, as in muscle tension pains, fibrositis, and just plain fatigue.

There are many methods of applying heat locally: via hot-water bottles, electric heating pads, hot towels, and heating lamps. Your pharmacy or surgical supply store is a good source for various types of hot packs; these are specially designed to be soaked in hot water and to hold heat for longer periods than, for example, a towel would. Other methods apply heat to the body overall: hot baths and tubs, steam baths, hot mud baths, and saunas. But a few words of caution are in order: Take care to avoid burning the skin, and use particular care if there is a reduced blood supply to the area being heated, for example when arteriosclerosis of the vessels to a leg is present. If you apply too much heat to the body, as in a hot tub that is excessively hot, the body temperature and oxygen consumption can rise, increasing the demands on the heart. Properly used, heat is an effective but temporary remedy. Improperly used, it can be injurious.

Cold

As you might have guessed, the effects of cold applications are opposite to those of heat. Where cold is applied, the blood vessels contract, blood flow is reduced, and the inflammatory reaction is dulled, which means that tissue swelling is reduced. Cold can also induce temporary analgesia, or pain reduction. Local applications of cold are most useful when inflammation first occurs, as with an acute and painful shoulder bursitis, when a muscle spasm grips the neck, or where the neck or shoulder girdle muscles have just been strained. Cold can be applied by various means: cold towels or ice packs. One convenient way of doing this is to purchase one or more of the cold packs sold for use in portable ice chests. These are readily available in sporting goods stores and can be cooled in the freezer to provide a nonmessy source of cold. Do not apply these packs to the skin directly, though, but use a towel or other insulating material as an interface.

As with heat, too much cold can have injurious effects. For one thing, cold applications can freeze the skin—especially where the blood supply has been diminished owing to poor circulation. Again, caution as well as common sense is indicated here.

In sum, heat and cold applications are temporary but effective and inexpensive methods of providing relief in certain soft-tissue rheumatic disorders. As usual, knowing what you are treating is your best guide to which one to try first.

THE LAYING ON OF HANDS

Massage is among the oldest forms of treatment used for the relief of musculoskeletal aches and pains. The Chinese used massage more than three thousand years ago, and it is the oldest known form of physical therapy. And from antiquity to the present practitioners have been enhancing the effectiveness of massage by preceding it with hot baths and the anointing of the body with oil.

Properly done, massage has many beneficial effects. It causes the muscles to relax and their nutrition to improve owing to an increase in blood flow. Muscles, scar tissue, and tendons are stretched, improving motion. The general overall effect on the body is one of sedation (a good alternative to drugs).

Many different types of massage are available, and most use one or more of four basic massage movements—stroking, compression (kneading), percussion (striking), and vibration. Perhaps the most popular type in this country is the "Swedish massage," which mainly uses a combination of the first three of these movements. The Japanese form of massage, known as *shiatsu,* is also becoming increasingly popular. The word is derived from the Japanese *shi,* meaning "finger," and *atsu,* meaning "pressure." Pressure on the muscles and other soft tissues is applied by the finger, elbow, or knee, and percussion is used as well. People who have experienced *shiatsu* generally agree that although not initially as soothing as a Swedish massage, this form often provides excellent temporary relief of localized pains and good muscle relaxation.

Innumerable variations of massage are available, even within the Swedish and *shiatsu* categories, each of which puts more or less emphasis on one or other of the four basic movements. It's worth noting, though, that a few adherents of "modern" massage, unfortunately, have pushed the techniques too far, to the point of actually bruising the skin. This has not been common, in my experience, but it's still worth being careful to avoid such "techniques."

It is possible for you to give yourself a massage, but not as effectively or as sedatingly as someone else can do it. It's pretty hard to relax while rubbing your own neck, for example. The next best thing, though, is to buy one of the handheld electric vibrating massagers that have a semi-firm ball of rubber on the end. Many of my patients have found these useful in relieving neck and shoulder girdle muscle tensions.

A few final words about massage. You'll experience the best results when you are able to relax and "flow with the tide." For various reasons many people are actually frightened of massage or consider it totally hedonistic or sinful. Perhaps some of these concerns stem from the publicized attempts of many cities to limit or eradicate the presence of "massage parlors" in their environs. I suggested once to a male patient that he get a massage, and I thought his wife was going to hit me. But it's not hard to find a legitimate masseur or masseuse and to avoid those that primarily offer other services.

MEDICATIONS

A limited number of nonprescription medications are available for the temporary relief of soft-tissue rheumatic aches and pains. They can be obtained in the forms of liniments or oral preparations. All have their proper use, and each differs significantly from the others. I will review each of them in turn. If you want more detailed descriptions of these medications, see *The Pharmacological Basis of Therapeutics* by Goodman and Gilman.[4]

LINIMENTS

A liniment is a preparation that is rubbed on the skin in order to relieve pain in deeper structures by counterirritation. It irritates the skin and decreases pain perception in other areas. The most widely used active substance in the many available liniments is methyl salicylate, which is also known as sweet birch oil, oil of wintergreen, gaultheria oil, and betula oil. Methyl salicylate has the very distinctive odor of wintergreen, which most people find quite pleasing. It is intended for external use only.

Methyl salicylate is most effective when applied to the skin over a painful soft-tissue area. It is not absorbed significantly into the bloodstream, so it has no actual effect on inflammation or metabolism of deep tissues beneath the skin and therefore provides only temporary pain relief. Liniments are often extremely helpful for this purpose and are a frequently overlooked form of therapy. Allergic reactions to methyl salicylate can occur, but they are rare.

Aspirin and Other Salicylates

Many forms of salicylates can be taken by mouth to relieve pain and irritation. The most significant by far is aspirin—acetylsalicylic acid. Aspirin is the standard by which all other analgesic and anti-inflammatory agents are measured. It has been said many times that if aspirin were discovered today it would be hailed as a wonder drug.

A precursor of aspirin, salicin, is present in the bark of willow, aspen, and poplar trees, and was used early in human history to combat fever. Some twenty-four hundred years ago, Hippocrates was aware of therapeutic uses of salicin. Salicylic acid was produced from derivatives of salicin in 1838 but was too toxic for oral use. Aspirin was actually first prepared in 1853 by Charles Gerhardt but was initially considered to be a medical curiosity. In 1874, chemists were able to prepare it from phenol and carbon dioxide. Although aspirin didn't become widely available until 1899, many of its therapeutic properties were known before that. The list of its beneficial effects might well surprise you.

To begin with, aspirin has a significant analgesic or pain-relieving effect. It reduces fevers effectively, reduces inflammation from many causes, has a mild anticoagulant effect (decreases blood clotting), and is widely used to help prevent heart attacks and strokes. Appropriate doses of aspirin increase the urinary output of uric acid and were once commonly used to treat the acute and chronic forms of gout. Small doses, however, can actually decrease the urinary excretion of uric acid, so people with a history of gout need to take aspirin with care.

Many people mistakenly believe that aspirin damages the heart. In the usual therapeutic doses, aspirin has no significant effect on the heart. In fact, it is one of the basic drugs used to treat the heart inflammation that occurs in rheumatic fever.

Aspirin is not without its adverse side effects, however, even in doses considered to be within the safe therapeutic range. One of the most common is gastric irritation, great enough at times to produce gastritis, peptic ulcers, and bleeding. Allergic reactions such as severe nasal congestion, asthma, and rash are uncommon but do occur. People taking anticoagulant medication should avoid using aspirin, since the latter can increase the risk of bleeding. In aspirin overdoses, increased respiration, metabolic abnormalities, confusion, temporary hearing loss, and dizziness may result.

Aspirin is available in tablets ranging from 65 to 650 milligrams, the most popular being 300 milligrams (5 grains). The usual adult dose is 600 milligrams (10 grains) every four hours, although somewhat higher doses may be tolerated.

In attempts to prevent stomach irritation that can occur with aspirin, pharmaceutical companies have produced other forms of salicylates, such as sodium salicylate, choline magnesium trisalicylate, and salicylsalicylic acid. The latter two are available only with a doctor's prescription. The three are more expensive than aspirin but have a place in the treatment of those who cannot tolerate aspirin.

Acetaminophen and Phenacetin

Acetaminophen was actually first used in medicine in 1893, but it did not become popular until 1949. It has been available without a prescription in the United States since 1955 and can be purchased under many trade names, such as Tylenol and Datril. The drug is about as effective as aspirin when used to treat fevers and pain. Unlike aspirin, however, it has no significant anti-inflammatory effects, which limits its usefulness in the treatment of many musculoskeletal disorders.

When taken in overdoses, acetaminophen can have serious damaging effects on the liver and kidneys. The conventional oral dose for adults is from 325 to 650 milligrams every four hours and should not be exceeded. Some authorities caution against the use of acetaminophen for more than ten days except on the advice of a physician.

Phenacetin is chemically related to acetaminophen. It is used primarily in combination with aspirin and caffeine (referred to as APC) or in combination with other drugs such as muscle relaxants or barbiturates. Overall, phenacetin is slightly more toxic than acetaminophen and is therefore less popular.

Ibuprofen

Ibuprofen is one of the nonsteroidal anti-inflammatory drugs (NSAID). It has been used in England and Europe since 1969 and has been available in the United States by prescription since 1974. In 1984, the Arthritis Advisory Committee of the Federal Drug Administration approved the nonprescription use of ibuprofen. It is now available under the trade names Advil and Nuprin.

More details of both the beneficial and the toxic effects of ibuprofen are given in the section on NSAIDs, but a few words are in order now. Ibuprofen has many effects similar to those of aspirin. It reduces fever and pain, and has significant anti-inflammatory properties. Many authorities believe that the drug has fewer side effects than aspirin. As a prescription drug it has been widely used to treat such disorders as arthritis, soft-tissue rheumatism, headaches, menstrual cramps, dental pains, and fever. Properly used it has been proven to be an effective drug. Its adverse side effects include allergic reactions (particularly in aspirin-sensitive people) such as asthma, rashes, and gastrointestinal irritation leading to stomach and duodenal ulcers.

At this writing, the recommended adult dose is one or two 200-milligram tablets every four to six hours, not to exceed six tablets in twenty-four hours without a doctor's approval. The smallest effective dose is always recommended. Pregnant women and people taking anticoagulant drugs are warned not to take ibuprofen, and other restrictions apply as well.

My own personal feelings are that ibuprofen is an effective NSAID, but I would include the caveat that, like *any other drug,* you should use ibuprofen with care, acquaint yourself with the manufacturer's recommendations, and monitor yourself when you take it for signs of possible side effects.

DIETS

Discussing the role of diet in health maintenance is somewhat akin to discussing politics or religion: No matter what you say, you're bound to raise someone's hackles. Still, the subject inevitably arises in a discussion such as this, so I must dare to enter the fray and discuss the role of diet in treating the soft-tissue rheumatic diseases.

Much has been written over the years on diet and the treatment of arthritis and rheumatism. The lists of recommended and proscribed foods have been lengthy and confusing. Fish diets, vegetable and fruit diets, macrobiotic diets, "natural food" diets—all have been posed as modes of treatment for musculoskeletal pain.

I have seen many patients embark on various dietary regimens in the hope of reducing or curing such disorders as tendinitis, fibrositis, and polymyalgia rheumatica, and the results have never been the least bit encouraging. I have never seen a specific pattern of food intake in this or any other country that warrants a medical recommendation; nor have I read any convincing literature to the contrary.

Clearly, a well-balanced diet is essential to our general health. Nor is there any question that certain foods can have adverse effects on our bodies. What cannot be inferred from such general statements is that soft-tissue rheumatism can be predictably prevented, reduced, or cured by eating or not eating certain foods, minerals, vitamins, or additives. Unfortunately, I can offer no proof to document this claim.

My only recommendations regarding diet and nutrition are that you reach and maintain your ideal weight and eat well balanced meals adequate in protein, carbohydrate, fat, minerals, vitamins, and fiber. Considerable research has been and continues to be done on nutrition and its relationship to disease, and I remain hopeful that dietary manipulation will be shown to benefit one or more of the soft-tissue rheumatic diseases. At this time, though, no such evidence is at hand.

SPAS

Sometimes it's difficult to take leave of your anxieties and stress-generated aches and pains when you're at home or on a harried vacation. For those with the time and money, a visit to a spa may be the answer. The right one can afford you the needed rest, relaxation, exercise, diet, pampering, and fresh outlook. Spas serve a definite need, and they've been popular for a few millennia.

In its strict sense, the word *spa* refers to a resort area where there are mineral spring waters held to be of medicinal value. In fact, the word derives from the village of Spa in eastern Belgium, long known for the supposed "curative" powers of its mineral springs. Today the term is used very broadly, and some think of it as any commercial enterprise with exercise rooms, hot tubs, saunas, and the like. I'm using the term in its older, more restrictive sense—as a resort area built around "the taking of the waters."

The ancient Romans took good advantage of hot mineral springs and built many bathhouses; two well-known ones are in Bath, England, and the Baths of Caracalla in Rome. Where they could find no natural hot springs, the Romans did the next best thing and created their own. One of the most dramatic I have seen is at Masada, built by Herod on a small plateau close to and thirteen hundred feet above the Dead Sea at the eastern edge of the Judean Desert. Masada was very elaborate, with remains of many frescoes and tile mosaics. It features both a hot house (caldarium) and a room for cold baths (frigidarium). This spa was fit for a king in its time and an exciting archaeological discovery.[5]

Today spas are available for those with budgets varying from modest to unlimited. Europe is best known for luxurious spas, evoked by such names as Baden-Baden in Germany, Karlovy Vary (Carlsbad) and Marianske Lazne (Marienbad) in Czechoslovakia, and Montecatini in Italy. Low-budget trips are available to these places, and you don't have to be wealthy to avail yourself of a real treat.

Asia is not without its many hot springs and spas. When I was in the army I had an opportunity to visit one of these areas, the spas in Beppu, Japan. As the boat pulled up to the dock, I could see people on the beach covered with sand heated by the springs that reached the shore. The hotels featured hot mineral baths and hot mud baths (known as *jigoku*, or "boiling hells") followed by a relaxing *shiatsu* massage.

Closer to home there's Hot Springs, Arkansas. It was there in 1541 that Hernando De Soto found what the local Indians had long known—bubbling hot springs gave relief to muscular aches and pains. Today the springs there continue to provide the same pleasant services. Others are in Desert Hot Springs, California, resorts in Aspen and Vail, Colorado, and many others across the United States.

There is no solid scientific evidence that mineral waters have special curative effects over any other water taken by mouth or applied externally. The benefits of spas seem to lie in their relaxing ambience.

If your muscle aches and pains are generated by tensions and anxieties, you might consider spending a week or two at a spa. You may be pleasantly surprised by taking advantage of what others have been doing over the last few thousand years.

CAUTION: WORTHLESS TREATMENTS AND CURES

Quackery is the misrepresentation of a remedy's true powers. The 32 million Americans currently suffering from arthritis and rheumatism are prime targets for inflated claims. The Arthritis Foundation estimates that the annual bill for unproved or quack remedies is about $950 million. This translates into $25 spent on worthless treatments and cures for every dollar going toward scientific research on rheumatic diseases.

Even such an apparent harmless "treatment" as a copper bracelet can take its toll if it delays your seeking effective therapy. Other bogus remedies can turn out to be far more dangerous than that. One of my patients once asked if it was safe to try some very nice smelling Chinese herb pills that her friends said were effective for their aches and pains. The label on the bottle listed only various herbs, most of which were unknown to me. I cautioned her against trying them. Three months later, a report from the University of California, San Francisco, revealed that four patients, one of whom died, had developed bone marrow depressions from these pills.[6] One of the ingredients that was not listed on the label proved to be phenylbutazone, a potent anti-inflammatory medication that can cause bone marrow depression and death. This drug has its place in the treatment of rheumatic diseases but only if monitored very carefully by a physician skilled in its use.

It is in your best interest to learn more about the many unproven, worthless, and often dangerous treatments that you are being exposed to. A good way to begin is to contact your local Arthritis Foundation office or the national office in Atlanta for more information.[7] You may save yourself a lot of grief and misery.

WHEN TO SEE YOUR DOCTOR

Having concerns about the significance of even mild aches and pains is reason enough to see your doctor. Often a patient will begin with, "I'm embarrassed to be here about such a minor pain." But if you're worried about something in your body, there is no reason at all to be embarrassed. If the pain proves to be minor, knowing that will help relieve your anxiety.

Many soft-tissue aches and pains are caused by disorders that last only a week or two. A mild muscle strain or the "flu," for example, may pass with little or no treatment. If your symptoms last more than two weeks, you should certainly consult your physician. If you suspect that you may have giant cell arteritis or reflex sympathetic dystrophy, as described in previous chapters, seek medical advice as soon as you can.

10

The Role of Your Doctor

BLENDING THE OLD AND THE NEW

A wide range of effective medical treatments for soft-tissue rheumatic diseases is available through your doctor. While I touched on many of them in previous chapters, here I focus on these medical treatments in detail. Some are simply sophisticated and efficient variations of treatments that have been used for millennia. The application of heat for pain relief is as old as recorded history, for example, but it has been improved by the use of diathermy and ultrasound, and cold can now be administered via coolant fluorimethane sprays.

New theories of pain perception have resulted in new treatment aids; for example, the transcutaneous nerve stimulator. And the discovery of the effectiveness of cortisone therapy in rheumatoid arthritis a little more than thirty years ago ushered in a new era of pharmacology, bringing with it many potent medications such as the nonsteroidal anti-inflammatory drugs.

Our new knowledge has resulted not only in new techniques and drugs but in a deeper understanding of the soft-tissue rheumatic diseases and accurate explanations of many aches and pains that long went undefined. We have come to realize, in turn, that certain disorders require not only the services of a physician but also the assistance of other professionals, such as physical therapists, pharmacologists, psychological counselors, and social workers, working in a "team" approach.

Before turning to specific medical treatments for soft-tissue rheumatism, let me emphasize again that some soft-tissue rheumatic diseases respond well to simple therapy, but others require medical treatment by trained personnel. You need a true diagnosis to tell the difference and active medical guidance in the latter instance. Still, even where medical treatment is necessary, your full understanding can only improve the situation. It's always important for us to remind ourselves—doctors and patients alike—that the effectiveness of medical treatment is always increased when the patient is a well informed, active participant.

PHYSICAL THERAPY

The goals and methods of physical therapy (called physical medicine by some) are frequently misunderstood. Basically, physical therapy is based on physical methods, as the name implies. Simply put, it uses such techniques as the application of heat and cold, massage, muscle stretching and strengthening, and increasing the range of motion in joints to achieve the goal of rehabilitation. Physical therapy is not a "cure," and if patients view it as such and expect total pain relief, they are often disappointed. The great value of physical therapy in treating the soft-tissue rheumatic diseases lies in its ability to decrease pain and spasm temporarily and to improve the function and nutrition of the muscles and other soft tissues.

Only a well trained professional therapist is qualified to administer the many physical therapy methods available. Also, to be maximally effective, the therapy has to be individualized and often integrated with other forms of treatment. It is unreasonable, for example, to expect a few applications of heat and massage alone to cure a case of fibrositis or psychogenic rheumatism. Also, physical therapy methods can help to relieve the pain of a tennis elbow, but they won't prevent a recurrence unless the original factors behind the disorder are eliminated. Successful treatment of soft-tissue rheumatic diseases often requires many forms of therapy, and a doctor familiar with your case is in the best position to design and coordinate all the components of your treatment.

Physical therapy often plays a supporting role in the treatment of soft-tissue rheumatism. In disorders in the tendinitis group, for example, the temporary relief of pain and the improved function of the muscles and other soft tissues can certainly hasten recovery. In fibrositis and psychogenic rheumatism, physical therapy can also give temporary relief but only as part of a total treatment program. Polymyalgia rheumatica and giant cell arteritis are treated primarily with prednisone but, again, physical therapy can aid in recovery if muscles have become weak. The reflex sympathetic dystrophies require intensive and at times long-term physical therapy. Let's take a closer look at how a physical therapist might participate in the treatment of specific disorders.

Heat and Cold

Traditional and very effective methods of applying heat therapeutically are towels, packs, baths, saunas, and heat lamps. Heat delivered in these ways does not penetrate the skin very deeply, yet it can raise body temperature to an uncomfortable degree if used over a large part of the body for a prolonged period. A physical therapist, however, can apply heat to specific areas of the body in a controlled manner using other methods—infrared lamps, for instance. Another method—using short- and long-wave diathermy apparatuses—takes advantage of the heat produced by electromagnetic high-energy waves. A therapist might also administer high-frequency sound waves, which generate deep heat and can be applied via ultrasound machines. Again, the application of heat by any of these means cures nothing and is best used to give temporary relief of soft-tissue pains and muscle spasm. Its effectiveness must be weighed against its cost in determining if it should be used and, if so, how long it should be continued.

Cold

There are fewer techniques of administering cold than heat. Cold packs and cold towel compresses can give temporary relief of muscle spasm and inflammation. Some physicians and physical therapists spray the skin with a very rapidly evaporating liquid called fluorimethane. The evaporation causes rapid cooling of the skin, which can induce a reflex relaxation in underlying muscles. The technique is followed by gentle muscle stretching. There are strong proponents of this method, but I feel that the beneficial effects of the technique are somewhat overrated. Still, a brief trial might be worthwhile.

Massage and Range of Motion

I covered the beneficial effects of massage earlier. Massages can be administered by masseuses or masseurs, but in certain circumstances a physical therapist can combine massage with muscle stretching and maneuvers directed toward increasing the range of motion of joints stiffened by disuse or disease. The judicious application of these techniques hastens recovery from such disorders as frozen shoulder or reflex sympathetic dystrophy.

Muscle-Strengthening Exercises

It is surprising and at times disconcerting to see how rapidly a muscle can become weak if it is put at rest either voluntarily or because of a disease process. If the rest is prolonged, not only will the muscles grow weak but the bones in the area of the associated muscle attachments will lose calcium and become what is called *osteoporotic*. Physical therapists can play a very important role in prescribing and supervising exercises to strengthen muscle groups, improve range of motion in joints, loosen soft tissues that are tight, and help prevent calcium loss from bones. It's beyond the scope of this book to review the almost infinite varieties of strengthening exercises, but it's worth mentioning that any exercise program should reflect one important characteristic: It should be designed to let you do the important exercises at home. Exercising three times a week for a half hour at a physical therapist's office just isn't enough to return the tissues to function. But first you need to be instructed in your program, which should be developed by a physical therapist to meet your specific needs.

MEDICATIONS

As we have made clear, the number of available nonprescription medications is limited, but doctors have the option to choose treatments from larger, more diverse, and more potent groups of drugs. The drugs covered in this chapter are available legally in the United States only by prescription, and I believe wisely so. Many have the potential to produce serious side effects or to interfere with the effects of other medications. You should take them only as directed and always in the prescribed dose—never more. And to help avoid all preventable problems that could arise when your doctor prescribes a drug, make sure you tell him or her if you

- are allergic or have had undesirable reactions to any medicine, including aspirin;
- are taking any other prescription or nonprescription medication;
- have any other medical problem, such as (but not limited to) ulcers, bleeding disorders, or kidney disorders;
- are pregnant or plan to become pregnant while taking these medications;
- are breast feeding;
- suspect that you are having an undesirable side effect of the medication.

It is beyond the scope of this book to list all the possible uses, actions, precautions, interactions, and side effects of the medications I cover. If you have any questions regarding any medication or any symptom that arises while you are taking one, by all means consult your physician.

Categories of Drugs

If I listed the numerous medications available by prescription in alphabetic order and suggested you learn some basic facts about them, I suspect you would close this book and find something else to do. There's a simpler way and that is to group the available drugs into classes based on their actions and chemical structures. The great majority of drugs used to treat soft-tissue rheumatic diseases fall into five major categories: (1) pain relievers that have no significant anti-inflammatory action (the narcotic analgesics), (2) the salicylates, (3) the nonsteroidal anti-inflammatory drugs (NSAIDs), (4) the muscle relaxants, and (5) cortisone and its derivatives. Other, less common drugs are described under a sixth category headed "other medications."

Narcotic Analgesics with No Anti-Inflammatory Effects

The oldest known analgesics are the narcotics. The word *narcotic* is derived from the Greek word *narkotikos,* meaning torpor, or mental lethargy. Most of the narcotic analgesics used today are synthetically related derivatives of opium, which is found in the poppy plant *Papaver somniferum.* Opium is highly addicting, so chemists have changed its chemical structure in attempts to find drugs that are less addicting and dulling to the senses but that still give good pain relief. Of these, codeine is the most frequently prescribed. But codeine tends to cause nausea and constipation in many people and still has mild addictive properties, so other related drugs have been synthesized and made available, such as hydrocodone (Vicodin), propoxyphene (Darvon), and pentazocine (Talwin). These drugs all share the same effects to one degree or another. They are useful when pain relief is paramount but have no effect on inflammation. Aspirin or acetaminophen is sometimes added to codeine and similar drugs to enhance their effects. It is possible to build up a tolerance to or become addicted to these drugs if they are taken for a long time; in this case larger and larger amounts become needed to achieve the same pain-relieving effect. Clearly, then, narcotics should be used sparingly and discontinued as soon as possible.

Salicylates

The best known salicylate is, of course, acetylsalicylic acid—aspirin. Besides their analgesic effect, the salicylates have a significant anti-inflammatory effect as well. Aspirin's major side effect, as we have said, is irritation of the stomach and duodenum. To prevent this problem, pharmacologists have altered aspirin to make such drugs as magnesium salicylate (Magan), choline magnesium trisalicylate (Trilisate), and salicylsalicylic acid (Disalcid). These substances, which are more expensive than aspirin, may be tolerated by an aspirin-sensitive stomach.

Nonsteroidal Anti-Inflammatory Drugs (NSAIDs)

A nonsteroidal anti-inflammatory drug is a substance that has the ability to suppress inflammation and that is unrelated to cortisone or its derivatives. Theoretically, this group includes aspirin and certain other salicylates, but the term generally is used to describe other classes of drugs. The first of these synthetic drugs, phenylbutazone (Butazolidin, Azolid), was introduced in 1949 and was followed by a related drug, oxyphenbutazone (Tandearil). Indomethacin (Indocin) was introduced in 1965. In 1974, ibuprofen (Motrin, Rufen) became available. After that the trickle of new NSAIDs introduced in the United States became a steady stream, with eight more following as of this writing, including the nonprescription Advil and Nuprin, as we have said. (One, zomepirac [Zomax], has been withdrawn from the market because of serious adverse side effects.) These drugs were initially designed to fight the pain and inflammation of arthritis, and further studies showed that many were useful in the treatment of soft-tissue rheumatic diseases such as tendinitis, bursitis, ligamentitis, and the like.

In general, these drugs are comparable to or slightly more effective than aspirin in anti-inflammatory effects, and some seem to have fewer side effects. Exceptions are phenylbutazone and oxyphenbutazone, which have serious effects on the bone marrow, and indomethacin, which is associated with a relatively high incidence of gastrointestinal irritation and central nervous system effects (such as headache and confusion). These substances have their place, particularly in the treatment of certain forms of arthritis, but anyone under treatment needs careful monitoring by a doctor. You can obtain further information on these drugs from your doctor or by reading the insert sheets that accompany the drugs. Also, the *Physician's Desk Reference* and standard textbooks on medical therapeutics are good reference sources and are available at most public libraries.

Regarding the soft-tissue rheumatic disorders, the NSAIDs are most useful in treating the tendinitis group of inflammations and generally are much less effective in treating fibrositis and reflex sympathetic dystrophy. Polymyalgia rheumatica and giant cell arteritis are best treated with prednisone.

The NSAIDs currently available by prescription are

- Diflunisal (Dolobid)
- Fenoprofen (Nalfon)
- Ibuprofen (Motrin, Rufen)
- Indomethacin (Indocin)
- Meclofenamic acid (Meclomen)
- Naproxen (Naprosyn)
- Oxyphenbutazone (Tandearil)
- Phenylbutazone (Butazolidin)
- Piroxicam (Feldene)
- Sulindac (Clinoril)
- Tolmetin (Tolectin)

Muscle Relaxants

The drugs used as "muscle relaxants" do not really relax the muscles directly. Rather, they generate relaxation indirectly through a combination of analgesia, sedation, and other factors that affect the nervous system. Muscle relaxants have no effect on inflammation and are used as adjuncts to rest, physical therapy, and other measures solely for the relief of the discomfort associated with acute painful musculoskeletal conditions.

My experience with these drugs suggests that they may be helpful for a week or two but are of limited use in the prolonged treatment of any soft-tissue rheumatic disorder. Doses needed to produce any significant muscle relaxation often have undesirable side effects on the nervous system, such as drowsiness and dizziness. Again, these substances have a place, but I personally feel that prolonged use should be avoided. Drugs in this group are

- Carisoprodol (Soma)
- Chlorzoxazone (Paraflex)
- Cyclobenzaprine (Flexeril)
- Diazepam (Valium)
- Metaxalone (Skelaxin)
- Methocarbamol (Robaxin)
- Orphenadrine citrate (Norflex)

One other drug different from those above deserves mention: quinine. Quinine is a derivative of the cinchona bark and is best known for its antimalarial properties. It has been used for centuries, and its effects on malaria were well known to the Amazonian aborigines. In addition, it has been found to be effective frequently in relieving the leg muscle cramps that occur at night. Quinine should *not* be used by pregnant women, since it can cause damage to the fetus. It is the quinine in quinine water that gives your gin and tonic that distinctive taste. Quinine is available without prescription in a 300-milligram capsule dose.

Cortisone and Its Derivatives

Cortisone and its derivatives have revolutionized the treatment of hundreds of diseases, including the rheumatic ones. It is difficult to picture practicing modern medicine without them. Their use in musculoskeletal, heart, gastrointestinal, lung, kidney, blood, skin, eye, ear, and nervous system disorders and cancer treatment has become legendary.

Cortisone is one of the hormones secreted by the cortex of the adrenal glands, which lie directly above the kidneys. It is one of a group of hormones known variably as corticosterones, adrenocortical hormones, or simply "steroids." These hormones play essential roles in protein, carbohydrate, and salt metabolism. When given in doses larger than normally found in the body, cortisone is a potent suppressor of both inflammation and the body's immune response. These effects form the basis for its use in the treatment of the rheumatic diseases.

During my medical training I was both fortunate and privileged to study with Drs. Philip S. Hench, Howard F. Polley, and Charles H. Slocumb, who played major roles in one of the great milestones in medical history: the discovery of the value of cortisone in the treatment of rheumatoid arthritis. The story of cortisone has been well told in two articles in the *Mayo Clinic Proceedings*[1,2] by Drs. Polley and Slocumb, and I'd like to share a portion of it here.

In 1933, in Rochester, Minnesota, after almost twenty years of effort, Dr. Edward C. Kendall isolated cortisone, originally called compound E, from beef adrenals. The drug's physiologic effects were investigated there and in other laboratories in this country, but because cortisone could be produced in only tiny amounts, these investigations were limited and many effects of the substance remained unknown. In May 1941, the urgency of the study suddenly escalated: A national conference on the adrenal gland was held because persistent rumors had it that German scientists had made an extract of the gland that supposedly allowed Luftwaffe pilots to fly at forty thousand feet without the use of oxygen. It was further rumored that German submarines were being sent to Argentina to obtain supplies of beef adrenal glands. The National Research Council gave compound E the highest priority for investigation.

The rumors were never confirmed and when, after the war, the government lost interest in compound E, Merck & Co., Inc., who had the job of developing it, lost its federal subsidy for study. Despite the incredibly high production cost, however, the company kept making the compound and by spring 1948 had synthesized a total of 9 grams (slightly less than the weight of two nickels!).

While these pharmacological events were going on, Dr. Philip S. Hench was making important clinical observations on patients with rheumatoid arthritis. In 1929, Hench saw a Mayo Clinic patient whose rheumatoid arthritis remarkably improved after the onset of jaundice resulting from a liver disease. He then noted that other events such as pregnancy or surgery could also improve arthritis. He assumed that some elusive "substance X" was being produced in the body that was accounting for this beneficial effect. He postulated that it could be an increased hormone production, possibly one from the adrenal gland.

In 1948, Dr. Randall Sprague, an endocrinologist at the Mayo Clinic, received two of the nine precious grams of compound E for study in patients with Addison's disease, a deficiency in adrenal cortex production. Dr. Hench persisted with great difficulty in obtaining from Sprague a small amount to try in treating rheumatoid arthritis. The attitude of the endocrinologist was one of great skepticism: "What do you suppose they'll think of next?" he said.

On September 21, 1948, a rheumatoid arthritis patient was given the first dose of compound E. The results were very promising, and with the cooperation of Merck, Hench was able to obtain more compound E for additional clinical trials. He and his colleagues carried out their studies with a secrecy that would be almost impossible to reproduce today. The improvement in the patients with rheumatoid arthritis was dramatic. In April 1949, the preliminary results were announced at the weekly Wednesday evening scientific meeting of the staff of the Mayo Clinic. Dr. Howard Rusk, who was then an associate editor of the *New York Times,* had learned of the impending presentation through a chance encounter with a trainee from the Mayo Clinic a day before the meeting. Rusk sent William L. Laurence, science editor of the *New York Times,* to Rochester, allowing the *Times* to be the first to inform the world about the event.

In 1950, Drs. Hench and Kendall were awarded Nobel prizes in Stockholm for their efforts. For those with a historical interest, I highly recommend reading the fascinating details of the story of cortisone in the *Mayo Clinic Proceedings.*[1,2]

Where Steroids Are Used Cortisone has undesirable effects along with its anti-inflammatory effects. For instance, it causes the body to retain excess amounts of salt. Over the years chemists have synthesized many derivatives in order to find ones that are safer to use. Today, the most widely used steroids are prednisone for oral administration and prednisolone for local joint and soft-tissue injection. These are among the safer and certainly the least expensive derivatives available for the treatment of rheumatic diseases. Many others, such as hydrocortisone, dexamethasone, triamcinolone, betamethasone, and beclomethasone, are available for specialized uses.

Cortisone and its derivatives have acquired something of a Jekyll and Hyde reputation. In any large group of people you will invariably find someone who describes the effects of these medications as "miraculous" and others who proclaim "never, never take steroids—I've been told that they can kill you." It's important at this point to put steroid treatment into perspective. If you don't need them or it is known that your condition can be improved without them, stay away from them. (This is good advice for any medicine, I might add.) There are many soft-tissue disorders, however, that respond poorly, if at all, to anything but steroid treatment. In these situations your choice is to suffer or accept what are, in the cases where they occur, generally mild undesirable side effects. It is true that steroids can cause considerable damage to the body if used in high doses for prolonged periods of time, a fact that is discussed below. In essence, the doctor's choice of whether or not to use steroids must be based on the total anticipated benefit in the particular situation.

Steroid injections are used frequently in the treatment of disorders in the tendinitis group—at times as the first treatment choice and at others when the condition fails to respond to other methods. The amount of steroid injected is not large, and if injections are not made on a regular basis, there is no detectable undesirable effect on the body. Many physicians will use a mixture of prednisolone and a local anesthetic, such as lidocaine, in such an injection. This has two benefits: It reduces the discomfort of the injection and, if the area of inflammation is completely injected, results in almost immediate relief of pain. When the anesthetic wears off, usually in a few hours, some pain may return until the prednisolone has had a chance to reduce the inflammation. Injections often produce dramatic relief in localized soft-tissue inflammations, such as tennis elbow, bursitis or tendinitis of the shoulder, trochanteric bursitis, trigger finger, and the like. Complications such as thinning of the skin over the area of an injection or actual ruptures of tendons or ligaments have been reported, particularly following frequent injections in the same area. This is because steroids can suppress the growth of fibrous tissues that give strength and support. Also, with any type of injection there is a slight risk of infection. Overall, these complications are rare, and where indicated, steroid injections have an excellent safety record.

Pure fibrositis has not been shown to be associated with any type of inflammation, and from a theoretical standpoint steroids should be of no value. But many physicians feel that local injections of steroids into muscle "trigger points" can give some relief to fibrositis sufferers of pain and stiffness. My personal experience is that such injections are not particularly useful in such cases, and I rarely use them. And, again, pure psychogenic rheumatism is not an inflammatory disorder, and steroids have no place in its therapy.

Polymyalgia rheumatica and giant cell arteritis are highly responsive to oral steroid therapy, often very dramatically so. Despite the reluctance of many patients to take prednisone and despite their concerns about side effects, the usual response is one of great satisfaction with the decision to take it. Again, if the dose is carefully monitored and reduced when possible, side effects can be kept to a minimum.

The reflex sympathetic dystrophies may respond very well to oral steroid therapy, but the result is not as predictable as in polymyalgia rheumatica or giant cell arteritis. Fortunately, other forms of therapy are available for these disorders.

Side Effects The side effects of steroids are related to the roles these substances play in the body's metabolism and the type of steroid used. The larger the dose of steroid, the greater the risk of complications. One possible effect is the slowing down of connective tissue growth. This can result in the slow healing of injuries (particularly to the skin), easy bruising, and ulceration of the stomach and duodenum, as examples. Steroids can affect glucose metabolism such that they bring out latent diabetes mellitus or make it worse where it is present. They also cause varying degrees of salt retention and potassium loss, which may result in excess fluid retention. The effects on blood cells, tissue growth, and the immune system may predispose to infections or increase one that is present, for example tuberculosis. Long-term use can cause osteoporosis (loss of calcium from the bones). Many steroids cause an increased appetite, and weight gain is common on higher doses. Fat distribution changes, resulting in rounding of the face ("moon face").

The side effects listed, and others as well, can usually be kept at a minimum in the treatment of soft-tissue rheumatic diseases, since these conditions usually do not require continuing high doses. It goes without saying, of course, that if you are under treatment with steroids of any amount, you should follow your doctor's instructions carefully and consult with him or her at regular intervals.

Other Medications

In certain instances your doctor might prescribe medications that do not fall into the groups reviewed thus far. It is not feasible to review or even list the many drugs and combinations of drugs currently available, but some are used often enough to warrant our attention here.

Tricyclic Antidepressants Examples of the tricyclic antidepressants are amitriptyline (Elavil) and imipramine (Tofranil). These substances have antidepressant effects and are widely used for the treatment of various types of emotional depressive states. Also, they frequently exhibit a beneficial effect on pain perception in certain conditions such as fibrositis and psychogenic rheumatism. Exactly how they work is unknown, but they may affect norepinephrine and serotonin metabolism and neuron function. These medications have no significant effect on pain produced by acute injury or inflammation, or on inflammation itself. They have significant potential side effects and should be taken only under prescription.

Others Reserpine (Serpasil) is derived from the root of *Rauwolfia serpentina,* a tropical plant. The powdered root has been used for centuries in India for its tranquilizing effect on the mentally disturbed. Its use as a tranquilizer and antihypertensive medication in Western medicine began in 1953. Reserpine has also been effectively used for the treatment of reflex sympathetic dystrophy.

A group of medications known as the beta-adrenergic blockers selectively blocks the effects of one of the actions of adrenaline (epinephrine) on body tissues. The most widely used drug in this group is propranolol (Inderal). It is used for the treatment of many types of heart diseases, hypertension, and migraine headaches. It has also been used successfully in the treatment of some cases of sympathetic dystrophy.

OTHER KINDS OF TREATMENT

In this section we'll consider other modes of therapy useful with soft-tissue rheumatic diseases that are distinct from drug therapy. These methods range in origin from those used at least three thousand years ago to those developed and refined only recently. The first three—acupuncture, acupressure, and the transcutaneous electrical nerve stimulator—share a common denominator: All have the ability to alter our perception of pain without the use of drugs.

ACUPUNCTURE

The role of acupuncture, the ancient Chinese method of treating many illnesses, ranks among the most controversial issues in Western medicine. There are many conflicting reports about whether or not acupuncture truly has beneficial effects, which make it very difficult to form a clear opinion as to its value.

Regarding its background, the traditional Chinese theory of acupuncture relates to a complex interrelationship of cosmic forces of life energy involving primarily the Yin and Yang and twelve body channels or ducts. The Yin is considered to be the female principle, passive and dark and represented by the earth. The Yang is the male principle, active and light and represented by the heavens. The channels of the body are thought to be deeply set in the muscles, and their courses, or meridians, dictate the placement of acupuncture needles for treatment. There are more than one thousand sites on the body for inserting the long, thin needles. In ancient times the needles were made of flint, then of gold, then silver, iron, and steel. The insertion of the needles is thought to bring about a balance of the disordered forces of the Yin and Yang. For those interested, one of the best descriptions of the theories and uses of acupuncture in ancient Chinese medicine appears in *The Yellow Emperor's Classic of Internal Medicine* by Ilza Veith.[3] It goes without saying that the theory as to why acupuncture is effective, the Chinese concept of cosmic forces, is at odds with the scientific concepts of orthodox Western medicine.

We know from the writings of Dr. Silas Weir Mitchell, introduced earlier, that acupuncture was used in this country during the American Civil War. But it really gained its greatest momentum in the United States after former President Richard M. Nixon's visit to China in 1972. Many people feel that modern Western medicine has not granted this technique the attention it deserves. I consider this criticism unfounded. I did a computerized search of the major medical journals in the world, most of which are from this country and Europe, and found that acupuncture-related articles numbered 173 from 1966 through 1972; 1,396 from 1973 through 1979; and 1,020 from 1980 to the time of this writing in 1984. Clinical trials of acupuncture have been performed in many of the major medical centers in this country.

But is acupuncture of value in the treatment of soft-tissue rheumatic diseases? All I have read, heard, and seen makes me believe that in certain individuals acupuncture can definitely give relief of pain—at times temporarily and at other times more permanently. In other people, though, it has no beneficial effect, and it is difficult if not impossible to predict with any precision who will benefit. I know of no statistics to help in even predicting what percentage of people will be helped, although I suspect that the percentage is not great, at least in this country. The ability of acupuncture to reduce any type of soft-tissue inflammation has yet to be proven, in my opinion. The value of the technique at best appears to be restricted to some hope of pain reduction.

Assuming that acupuncture relieves pain in some individuals, the next question is, How does it work? Many people who have had experience with the results of acupuncture therapy in both China and this country seem to agree that it works better in China. This had led many investigators to believe that it has a placebo effect—namely, that it works "in the mind" and depends heavily on the beliefs of the individual and the culture in which he or she lives. Considering the fact that the Chinese have performed open abdominal surgeries with anesthesia using acupuncture alone, it is hard to believe that it is only a placebo. I certainly have no answer to the question, but one may emerge as we gain a more precise knowledge of the soma-psyche-environment relationships involved in the perception of pain.

There are some possible complications of acupuncture—for example, the inadvertent puncture of a lung, nerve trunk, or blood vessel. There have been reports of bacterial infections and hepatitis from contaminated needles. However, when administered by a well trained practitioner who sterilizes the needles, acupuncture's side effects appear to be relatively rare.

Acupressure

Acupressure is an outgrowth of Chinese acupuncture and has been widely used by the Japanese in various forms of *shiatsu* (discussed earlier). Instead of the insertion of needles, as in acupuncture, pressure is applied over many defined soft-tissue sites or "points." There is an increasing interest in its use in this country as a form of massage. Again, acupressure can offer some temporary relief of the pain and discomfort of tense muscles and should be considered one of the many forms of physical therapy, not as a comprehensive treatment program.

Transcutaneous Electrical Nerve Stimulator (TENS)

The transcutaneous electrical nerve stimulator (TENS) is an electronic instrument used for the treatment of chronic pain. It is about the size of a cigarette pack and, powered by two small flashlight batteries, generates electrical pulses whose intensity and frequency can be varied. The electrical pulses are applied by one or two sets of electrodes taped to the skin, usually over the areas of pain. Relief of pain comes not from any effect on the underlying illness but probably from the stimulation of those nerve fibers that suppress our perception of pain.

The TENS has been helpful in many cases involving chronic pain. It has been used in treating some localized soft-tissue rheumatic disorders, but not commonly, since other methods are generally more effective.

Surgery

Surgical procedures are sometimes used to treat disorders in the tendinitis group. The carpal tunnel syndrome, for example, usually responds extremely well to surgical removal of the carpal ligament, and this operation is common. Recalcitrant tendinitis, scarred tendons, large collections of calcium in bursas, and Dupuytren's contracture all may be improved by surgery. In polymyalgia rheumatica and giant cell arteritis, surgery is used primarily for diagnostic purposes, in the form of a biopsy of a small artery to determine whether the artery is indeed inflamed. These two diseases are treated by medication. Many cases of reflex sympathetic dystrophy have been successfully treated by the surgical removal of groups of nerve cells known as the sympathetic ganglia.

Fibrositis and psychogenic rheumatism are neither diagnosed nor treated by surgical procedures.

Counseling

As I have frequently pointed out in this book, the hallmark of soft-tissue rheumatic diseases is pain—or at least some form of discomfort—that is invariably influenced by complex soma-psyche-environment relationships. This body-mind-nature interaction, to put it in different words, is hardly a new concept and has long been stressed in such ancient cultures as the Chinese and, to various degrees, by our own culture as well. Until science can explain precisely these complex relationships that affect our feelings and perceptions, the courses we take to obtain pain relief must at times be practical. That is, we must depend on what works rather than on what theoretically should work.

As I have noted elsewhere, certain soft-tissue rheumatic disorders such as fibrositis and psychogenic rheumatism may not respond to any drug or physical therapy measure. Also, in some disorders, such as those in the tendinitis group or reflex sympathetic dystrophy, the pain that individual sufferers experience may be unaccountably severe. In such situations your doctor may suggest either an evaluation or actual counseling and treatment by a psychologist or psychiatrist, since the psyche could be playing a significant part in your disorder. An evaluation of the mind-body relationship in your situation might be just as necessary as any laboratory or X-ray studies.

Epilogue

Where do we stand now in the battle against soft-tissue rheumatism? Over the past century, medical science has made ever-increasing progress in recognizing, classifying, and understanding the causes of the rheumatic disorders that affect our muscles and joints. And in the past few decades the proliferation of effective therapies has been nothing short of dramatic. Public education programs on the rheumatic illnesses are to be found all over the country. But the emphasis in these efforts is still on the arthritic diseases. The soft-tissue rheumatic disorders continue to be overshadowed and even ignored although they are among the most common medical causes of work loss, disability, and pain—and although they can be effectively treated.

In medical schools and research centers a similar pattern prevails: Arthritis draws the interest and attention, and soft-tissue rheumatism remains in the background. To confirm this fact one need only attend a review of the presentations made at any major rheumatological meeting in any part of the world. In proportion to their medical and social impact, the soft-tissue rheumatic diseases receive hardly any attention at all.

And yet we can remain optimistic. All the resources exist to reduce the human misery caused by soft-tissue rheumatic diseases. What we really need is a greater public awareness of the conditions and their therapies, since as I have shown these disorders are treatable even where they are not curable, but too often they go completely unrecognized. Were medical schools routinely to emphasize soft-tissue rheumatism in their curricula, were funding agencies to recognize the need for research in this field, we might soon rid humanity of a vast proportion of its aches and pains.

Word of mouth can be a powerful force, especially when the information in question can benefit everyone. In writing this book I hope I have gone some way toward spreading the word about soft-tissue rheumatism. Perhaps readers will find occasion to do the same—to mention the possibility of soft-tissue rheumatism to a pain sufferer or to a doctor or other medical professional. And those whose concern takes the form of letter writing or active participation might want to raise the issue of soft-tissue rheumatism with the National Arthritis Foundation. Let's keep talking until we get soft-tissue rheumatism out there where we can diagnose it, treat it, and—where we haven't succeeded yet—learn to cure it.

Glossary

acetaminophen A mild analgesic agent with no significant anti-inflammatory effect.

acetylsalicylic acid Aspirin.

Achilles' tendinitis An inflammation of the tendon that unites the calf muscle to the bony part of the heel.

acromioclavicular joint The joint where the clavicle (collar bone) meets the scapula (shoulder blade).

acupressure The application of pressure over specific soft tissue sites in order to relieve pain and muscle spasm.

acupuncture Ancient Chinese method of treating certain painful conditions by passing thin needles through the skin at specific points.

Addison's disease Disease resulting from a deficiency of hormone secretion from the adrenal cortex.

adhesive capsulitis A condition of severe pain and limitation of the shoulder joint resulting from inflammation of the joint capsule.

adrenal gland A small gland lying above the kidney that secretes cortisone, adrenaline, and related hormones.

adrenaline A hormone secreted by the adrenal medulla that stimulates the heart and blood vessels.

adrenocortical hormones A group of hormones secreted by the adrenal cortex, among which is cortisone.

alkaline phosphatase An enzyme found in liver and bone.

analgesic A drug that relieves pain.

anemia A condition in which there is a reduction of the red blood cells in the circulation. The red blood cells are carriers of oxygen to the tissues.

angina pectoris Chest pain due to insufficient blood flow to the heart muscle.

anserine bursitis An inflammation of the bursa that is located just below the knee on the inner side of the tibia.

arthralgia Joint pain in the absence of arthritis.

arthritis From the Greek word *arthron* meaning joint and the suffix *-itis* meaning inflammation. It generally means damage to a joint from any cause, such as infection, trauma, or inflammation.

arthrogram An X-ray picture of a joint taken after injecting an opaque dye into the joint.

articular cartilage Cartilage lining a joint.

articulation A union between bones; a joint.

ASA Abbreviation for acetylsalicylic acid; aspirin.

aspirin A chemical compound known primarily for its ability to reduce pain, fever, and inflammation.

autonomic nervous system The part of the nervous system that is concerned with involuntary function.

Baker's cyst See popliteal cyst.

bicipital tenosynovitis Inflammation of the long head of the biceps tendon.

biopsy Surgical excision of a small piece of tissue for diagnostic purposes.

bone A specialized form of calcified connective tissue.

bursa A small sac containing a sticky fluid that is interposed between muscles and tendons, or tendons and bony prominences.

bursitis Inflammation of a bursa.

calcium An element essential for bone growth and metabolism.

capsulitis Inflammation of a joint capsule.

carpal tunnel syndrome Pain, tingling, or numbness in one or more of the first four fingers of the hand resulting from pressure on the median nerve at the wrist.

cartilage A translucent, firm, elastic tissue. It is present in many joints as well as other structures, such as the nose and ear.

CAT scan See computerized axial tomography.

causalgia Intense burning pain.

chondritis Inflammation of a cartilage.

claudication Cramping of a muscle due to insufficient blood supply.

codeine A narcotic analgesic.

computerized axial tomography A specialized X-ray technique allowing visualization of sections of body tissue.

cortisone A hormone that is produced by the cortex of the adrenal gland. It can be produced synthetically. It has many effects on the body, including a potent anti-inflammatory one.

costochondritis Inflammation of a cartilage lying between a rib and the sternum (breast bone).

counterirritation Irritating the skin in order to relieve pain in deeper structures.

cranial arteritis See giant cell arteritis.

Cushing's syndrome A disorder resulting from overproduction of glucocorticoids from the adrenal gland.

degenerative arthritis See osteoarthritis.

De Quervain's tenosynovitis Inflammation of a tendon just proximal to the base of the thumb.

diathermy The therapeutic use of high-frequency currents to produce heat within parts of the body.

disease A pathological condition of the body; literally, the lack of ease.

disorder A pathological condition of the body or mind.

diuretic A drug that increases the flow of urine.

Dupuytren's contracture A contracture, or scarring down, of the fascia of the palm.

empirical treatment Treatment based on experience rather than scientific principles.

epicondylitis Inflammation of the tendon attachments to the epicondyles of the elbow; for example, tennis elbow.

epinephrine See adrenaline.

erythrocyte sedimentation rate See sedimentation rate.

ESR Abbreviation for erythrocyte sedimentation rate.

estrogens The female sex hormones.

fascia A fibrous membrane covering, supporting, or separating muscles.

fasciitis Inflammation of the fascia.

fibrositis A noninfectious condition characterized by muscle stiffness and pain and with no associated abnormal X ray or laboratory findings.

fluorimethane spray A rapidly evaporating coolant spray.

frozen shoulder See adhesive capsulitis.

genetic predisposition A susceptibility to a specific disease because of a person's genetic characteristics.

giant cell arteritis A condition characterized by inflammation of the arteries and associated with a variety of symptoms, including muscle pain and stiffness, high fevers, and blindness.

glucocorticoids A group of hormones secreted by the adrenal cortex, with effects on protein and carbohydrate metabolism, and important in fighting stress and inflammation; for example, cortisone.

golfer's elbow Pain on the inner aspect of the elbow. Medically known as medial epicondylitis.

gonorrhea An infection most commonly transmitted by sexual contact.

gout A hereditary metabolic disease of uric acid, characterized by acute arthritic inflammation.

hard tissues The bony tissues and the joints.

heart attack A condition caused by occlusion, or blockage, of the blood vessels supplying the heart muscle.

heel spurs Bony projections from the calcaneus, or heel bone, often associated with plantar fasciitis.

herniated disc Rupture of a disc between two vertebrae, often causing compression of a nerve and pain along its distribution.

hormone A substance produced by an organ or gland that is carried by the blood to other organs that are stimulated by that substance.

Horton's disease See giant cell arteritis.

hyper- A prefix meaning excessive.

hypo- A prefix meaning less than or a lack of.

hypothyroidism A disorder resulting from a lack of thyroid hormone.

ibuprofen An NSAID.

immunologic disease A disease caused or perpetuated by an imbalance of antibody defenses; for example, systemic lupus erythematosus.

incidence Frequency of occurrence over a period of time and in relation to the population in which it occurs.

indomethacin An NSAID.

infarction Death of a tissue due to an interruption of its blood supply.

inflammation The reaction of tissues to injury from any number of causes, such as infection or trauma. Characterized by varying degrees of warmth, redness, swelling, and pain.

infrared lamp A lamp producing heat rays beyond the red end of the light spectrum.

ischial bursitis A bursitis in the area of the ischial bones, upon which we sit. Also known as "weaver's bottom."

joint The part where two bones are joined. There are many types of joints. Some allow motion, others do not.

joint capsule The fibrous band of tissue encapsulating a joint.

joint space The space enclosed by the joint tissues and containing synovial fluid.

lateral epicondylitis See tennis elbow.

lidocaine One of many injectable compounds available that produce temporary local anesthesia.

ligament A band of strong fibrous tissue connecting the bones, cartilages, and other structures that support parts of the body.
ligamentitis Inflammation of a ligament.
liniment A liquid containing a medication applied to the skin.
lupus erythematosus See systemic lupus erythematosus.

massage A technique utilizing kneading, pressure, friction, and vibration, usually applied to the body to produce muscle relaxation.
medial epicondylitis See golfer's elbow.
median nerve compression syndrome See carpal tunnel syndrome.
menopause The period marking the end of menstrual activity. It is associated with a marked decrease in estrogen production.
meralgia paresthetica A disorder of sensation of the lateral area of the thigh, at times associated with pain. Due to injury of a nerve.
methyl salicylate A compound commonly used in liniments to produce counterirritation; also known as oil of wintergreen.
muscle A tissue in the body that has the special ability to contract or shorten.
myalgia Tenderness or pain in the muscles. Muscular rheumatism.
myocardial infarction See heart attack.
myofascial pain syndrome See fibrositis.
myositis Inflammation of muscle tissue.

narcotic A drug that relieves pain and produces various degrees of stupor and sleep.
nerve A group of specialized fibers that conducts impulses from one part of the body to another.
nerve entrapment syndrome A condition of varying degrees of loss of sensation, tingling, and pain produced by pressure on a nerve.
neuralgia Sharp, severe pain along the course of a nerve.
neurosis One of a disorder of thought processes not related to demonstrable disease of the nervous system and probably due to unresolved emotional conflicts. Contact with reality is maintained.
nonsteroidal anti-inflammatory drug A drug that suppresses inflammation in the body and is not related to cortisone or its derivatives.
NSAID Abbreviation for nonsteroidal anti-inflammatory drug.
nuisance condition Minor aches and pains that cause no significant disability or suffering.

olecranon bursitis Inflammation of the bursa at the elbow.
osteoarthritis A chronic disease involving the joints and characterized by destruction of cartilage and bony overgrowth.

osteoarthrosis Osteoarthritis of the spine.

osteoporosis A condition of loss of calcium from the bone, resulting in weakening of the bone structure and a predilection for fractures.

parathyroid hormone A hormone produced by small glands adjacent to the thyroid. It is essential to the proper function of calcium metabolism.

Parkinson's disease A chronic disease of the nervous system manifested by tremor, muscular weakness, and rigidity.

patella The kneecap.

phantom limb pain Pain perceived in a limb that has been amputated.

phenacetin An analgesic drug that has become less popular because of its deleterious side effects on the kidney.

phenylbutazone A nonsteroidal anti-inflammatory drug. A dangerous potential side effect is bone marrow depression.

physical therapy Rehabilitation concerned with restoration of function and prevention of disability following injury or disease, and utilizing physical methods such as heat, cold, exercise, range of motion, and muscle strengthening.

plantar fasciitis Inflammation of the plantar fascia, most commonly where it attaches to the calcaneus, or heel bone.

polymyalgia rheumatica A condition affecting primarily those over the age of fifty and characterized by shoulder and hip girdle muscle pain and stiffness and a high sedimentation rate.

popliteal cyst A swelling behind the knee caused by a disorder within the knee joint.

post-herpetic neuralgia Persistent pain following an infection of a nerve by herpes zoster, or "shingles."

potassium A mineral that is essential to muscle function.

prednisolone A derivative of cortisone that is commonly injected to produce local anti-inflammatory effects.

prednisone A derivative of cortisone and a hormone with potent anti-inflammatory effects.

prevalence The number of cases of a disease present in a specific population at a given time.

prognosis A prediction of the outcome of a disease and an estimate of the chance for recovery.

propranolol One of many drugs that block certain effects of adrenaline.

psychological conversion reaction A neurosis wherein unconscious emotional impulses are converted into bodily symptoms.

psychosis A mental derangement causing loss of contact with reality.

psychosomatic Pertaining to the relationship of mind and body.

quackery Misrepresentation. Pretending to treat or cure disease.

range of motion The range or arc of motion of a joint.

reflex sympathetic dystrophy A condition affecting one or more of the upper and lower extremities, characterized by severe pain and swelling and aberrations of skin temperature, color, and perspiration.

rheumatic Pertaining to rheumatism.

rheumatism From the Greek word *rheumatismos* meaning "subject to a flux." It is a general term referring to conditions characterized by pain and stiffness of joints or muscles. It includes arthritis and soft-tissue rheumatism.

rheumatoid arthritis A form of arthritis characterized by inflammation, pain, and swelling of joints and muscular stiffness.

sedimentation rate Also called the "sed rate." A laboratory test that measures the rate, in millimeters per hour, that red blood cells fall in a thin tube of blood. It is a nonspecific test in that a high rate may indicate inflammation or the presence of abnormal blood proteins. Two different methods are in general use; the Westegren method gives higher readings than the Wintrobe method.

self-limited disease A disease that even without treatment runs a definite course and subsides within a limited time.

sensory nerve A nerve that carries sensations such as heat, cold, vibration, and pain.

shiatsu A form of massage; from the Japanese *shi* (finger) and *atsu* (pressure).

shin splints A painful condition of the shin, with many causes.

shoulder-hand syndrome A disorder characterized by shoulder pain and hand swelling. It may follow inflammation of the shoulder or a heart attack.

skeletal muscles The voluntary striated muscles that are involved primarily in movement of parts of the body.

SLE Abbreviation for systemic lupus erythematosus.

soft-tissue rheumatism Pertaining to the many rheumatic conditions affecting the soft, as opposed to the hard or bony, tissues of the body.

soft tissues The muscles, tendons, ligaments, and the like, as opposed to the hard or bony tissues.

spasm An involuntary contraction of a muscle or group of mscles, associated with pain and interference of function.

sprain A joint injury causing tears in a ligament.

steroid Any one of a group of organic compounds, including cortisone and its derivatives, containing a specific basic chemical ring structure.

strain Injury to a muscle, tendon, or fascia by overstretching. A "pull."

stress The result produced in the body when it is acted upon by forces that disrupt its equilibrium. The term is used commonly to denote a cause or an effect.

stroke The effects produced by disrupting the blood supply to a portion of the brain.

Sudeck's atrophy Wasting of a limb following reflex sympathetic dystrophy.

sympathetic dystrophies A term that broadly includes causalgia, reflex sympathetic dystrophy, and Sudeck's atrophy.

sympathetic ganglia A group of nerve cells in the sympathetic division of the autonomic nervous system that function somewhat like "junction boxes."

syndrome A collection of symptoms and physical findings that characterize a particular abnormal condition or disease.

synovial fluid The sticky lubricating fluid found within a joint.

synovitis Inflammation of the synovium.

synovium A thin membrane of cells lining a joint.

systemic lupus erythematosus A chronic inflammatory disease of the connective tissue that affects the skin, heart, kidneys, joints, and other body organs. Its cause is unknown but thought to be closely related to a disorder of the body's immunological system.

temporal arteritis See giant cell arteritis.

tendinitis (or **tendonitis**) Inflammation of a tendon.

tendon A cord of dense fibrous connective tissue uniting a muscle to a bone.

tendon sheath A fibrous sheath surrounding a tendon and confining it to a bony groove.

tennis elbow Pain in the outside part of the elbow where a tendon attaches. Medically known as lateral epicondylitis.

tenosynovitis Inflammation of a tendon sheath.

TENS Abbreviation for transcutaneous electrical nerve stimulator.

testosterone The male sex hormone.

thyroid hormone The hormone produced by the thryoid gland. A decreased production causes the slowing of metabolism in many body tissues, causing symptoms that may include muscle stiffness and cramping.

tissue A collection of similar cells that act together to perform a certain function in the body. The primary tissues are epithelial (skin), connective, skeletal, muscular, and nervous.

transcutaneous electrical nerve stimulator An electronic device that produces a pulsating electrical current that is applied to the skin in order to relieve pain. The frequency and amplitude of the current can be controlled. Its abbreviation is TENS.

traumatic arthritis Arthritis that is a direct result of trauma or injury to a joint.

tricyclic antidepressant drug A drug of a specific chemical structure that has the ability to relieve mental depression. It may also have a beneficial effect on the perception of pain.

trigger finger A "snapping" of the finger on motion, usually caused by an inflammatory disorder of a tendon and its sheath.

trochanteric bursitis Inflammation of a bursa that lies near the hip joint.

ultrasound High-frequency inaudible sound waves. Used for therapeutic purposes, such as the production of heat in deep body tissues, or for diagnostic purposes in ultrasonography.

uric acid One of the body's waste products. An excess may lead to the condition of gout.

weaver's bottom Ischial bursitis.

Notes

CHAPTER 1

[1]In 1980, the estimated resident population of the United States was 226,504,825 (Department of Commerce, Bureau of the Census). In 1979, the National Center for Health Statistics, a branch of the U. S. Department of Health and Human Services, did various surveys of the health status of our population. The center estimated that 157.7 persons per 1,000 population suffered from either arthritis, bunion, synovitis, bursitis, tenosynovitis, or gout. This translates into a total of approximately 36 million persons in this country with these disorders—more than one out of every seven people suffering from either arthritis or soft-tissue rheumatism! (These figures *do not* include those suffering from fibrositis, polymyalgia rheumatica, giant cell arteritis, or reflex sympathetic dystrophy!) From the *National Health Interview Survey: United States, 1979 (Series 10, no. 136), DHHS Publication number (PHS) 81–1564, pp. 34–35, April 1981.*

In November 1977, an interesting report entitled "Tension Myalgia" appeared in the journal *Mayo Clinic Proceedings* (H. H. Stonnington, "Tension Myalgia," *Mayo Clinic Proceedings,* 52:75). It reviewed the incidence of soft-tissue rheumatism seen in the outpatient practice of the Mayo Clinic Department of Physical Medicine and Rehabilitation. In 1976, a total of 20,995 different cases had been treated (representing a broad spectrum of diseases in addition to arthritis and rheumatism). About one out of every three of those patients was diagnosed as having soft-tissue rheumatism. To quote from the article: "This means that 31 percent (6,529 patients) of the outpatient practice was devoted to chronic tendinomuscular problems that had nothing to do with arthritis, myositis, radiculopathy, fracture, and the like." Further, they stated, "Although these syndromes are vague, they are probably one of the most important causes of morbidity and work absenteeism."

In 1981, 1982, and 1983, reports regarding the types of arthritis and rheumatism seen in three rheumatology offices appeared in the official journal of the American Rheumatism Association. The reported incidence of soft-tissue rheumatic problems was 14, 35, and 27 percent, respectively. (A. Bohan, "The Private Practice of Rheumatology: The First 1,000 Patients," *Arthritis and Rheumatism,* 24:1304, 1981; D. J. Mazanec, "First Year of a Rheumatologist in Private Practice," *Arthritis and Rheumatism,* 25:718, 1982; and D. Alarcon-Segovia, F. Ramos Niembro, and R. F.

Gonzalez-Amaro, "One Thousand Private Rheumatology Patients in Mexico City," *Arthritis and Rheumatism,* 26:688, 1983.)

A report from a rheumatology clinic of the Peoria School of Medicine showed that in 285 new patients seen during 1979, fibrositis *alone* (a soft-tissue rheumatic disorder) was the second most frequent diagnosis (20 percent), exceeded only by osteoarthritis (29 percent). In patients under age fifty, fibrositis was the most common diagnosis (33 percent). These figures do not include the various other forms of soft-tissue rheumatism. (M. Yunus, A. T. Masi, J. J. Calabro, and I. K. Shah, "Primary Fibromyalgia," *American Family Physician,* 25:115, May 1982.)

Discussions among my colleagues reflect similar results: About one-third of the disorders seen in their rheumatology practices are those in the soft-tissue rheumatic group.

CHAPTER 4

[1]A. Bohan, "The Private Practice of Rheumatology: The First 1,000 Patients," *Arthritis and Rheumatism,* 24(1981):1304–1307.

[2]D. J. Mazanec, "First Year of a Rheumatologist in Private Practice," *Arthritis and Rheumatism,* 25(1982):718–719.

[3]D. Alarcon-Segovia, F. Ramos Niembro, and R. F. Gonzalez-Amaro, "One Thousand Private Rheumatology Patients in Mexico City," *Arthritis and Rheumatism,* 26(1983):688.

[4]M. Yunus, A. T. Masi, J. J. Calabro, and I. K. Shah, "Primary Fibromyalgia," *American Family Physician,* 25(1982):115–121.

[5]W. R. Gowers, "Lumbago: Its Lessons and Analogues," *British Medical Journal,* 1(1904):117–121.

CHAPTER 5

[1]Aristophanes, *The Birds* (414 B.C.) 1. 375.

[2]M. A. Kapusta and S. Frank, "The Book of Job and the Modern View of Depression," *Annals of Internal Medicine,* 86(1977):667–672.

[3]Many studies have been done among army and civilian patients to determine the relative incidence of the various causes of rheumatic complaints. Psychogenic rheumatism was found to rank with osteoarthritis and rheumatoid arthritis as a leading cause of musculoskeletal pains. During World War II, a study of 450 soldiers admitted to an army hospital with rheumatic complaints showed that 34 percent actually had psychogenic rheumatism (E. W. Boland, "Arthritis and Allied Conditions in an Army General Hospital," *California and Western Medicine,* 40(1944):7–9. Every individual in that group had been previously diagnosed erroneously as having an organic illness, usually arthritis. The total experience in United States Army rheumatism centers during World War II revealed that one of every seven soldiers previously diagnosed as having arthritis was actually disabled by psychogenic rheumatism (P. S. Hench and E. W. Boland, "The Management of Chronic Arthritis and Other Rheumatic Diseases among Soldiers of the United States Army," *Annals of Internal Medicine,* 24(1946):808–825. In 1948, a study of five hundred civilian patients with rheumatic complaints showed that 13.4 percent had psycho-

genic rheumatism (C. A. H. Watts, "The Mild Endogenous Depression," *British Medical Journal,* 1(1957):4. Many other studies have confirmed the high incidence of emotionally induced musculoskeletal pains (H. Merskey and F. G. Spear, *Pain: Psychological and Psychiatric Aspects,* Bailliere, Tindall and Cassell, London, 1967; J. W. Baker and H. Merskey, "Pain in General Practice," *Journal of Psychosomatic Research,* 10(1967):383; and R. A. Sternbach, *Pain: A Psychophysiologic Analysis* (New York: Academic Press, 1968).

Chapter 6

[1]K. A. Huston, G. G. Hunder, J. T. Lie, et al. "Temporal Arteritis—A 25-Year Epidemiologic, Clinical and Pathologic Study," *Annals of Internal Medicine,* 80(1978):162–167.

[2]T. Chuang, G. G. Hunder, D. M. Ilstrup, and L. T. Kurland, "Polymyalgia Rheumatica: A 10-Year Epidemiologic and Clinical Study," *Annals of Internal Medicine,* 97(1982):672–680.

[3]J. Hutchinson, "Diseases of the Arteries: On a Peculiar Form of Thrombotic Arteries of the Aged Which Is Sometimes Productive of Gangrene," *Archives of Surgery* (London), 1(1890):323–329.

[4]B. T. Horton, T. B. Magath, and G. E. Brown, "An Undescribed Form of Arteritis of the Temporal Arteries," *Proceedings of the Staff Meetings of the Mayo Clinic,* 7(1932):700–701.

[5]W. Bruce, "Senile Rheumatic Gout," *British Medical Journal,* 2(1888):811–813.

[6]H. S. Barber, "Myalgic Syndrome with Constitutional Effects," *Annals of the Rheumatic Diseases,* 16(1957):230–237.

[7]Joseph L. Hollander, M. D., ed., *Arthritis,* 7th ed. (Philadelphia: Lea & Febiger, 1966), p. 775.

[8]L. A. Healey, "Current Comment: Polymyalgia Rheumatica and the American Rheumatism Association Criteria for Rheumatoid Arthritis," *Arthritis and Rheumatism,* 26(1982):1417–1418.

Chapter 7

[1]S. W. Mitchell, C. R. Morehouse, and W. W. Keen, *Gunshot Wounds and Other Injuries of Nerves* (Philadelphia: Lippincott, 1864).

[2]R. L. Richards, "The Term 'Causalgia,' " *Medical History* (England), 11(1967):97–99.

[3]P. Sudeck, "Ueber die acute entzundliche Knochenatrophie," *Archiv Klinical Chirurgia,* 62(1900):147.

[4]S. W. Mitchell, *Injuries of Nerves and Their Consequences* (Philadelphia: Lippincott, 1872).

[5]S. W. Mitchell, *Wear and Tear: Or Hints for the Overworked* (Philadelphia: Lippincott, 8th ed., 1897).

[6]Mitchell, *Injuries,* pp. 195–201.

[7]*Ibid.,* p. 272.

[8]*Ibid.,* p. 295.

[9]*Ibid.*, p. 268.

[10]T. J. Pak, G. M. Martin, J. L. Magness, and G. Kavanaugh, "Reflex Sympathetic Dystrophy: Review of 140 Cases," *Minnesota Medicine,* 53(1970):507–512.

CHAPTER 9

[1]*Small Business Speaks: The Chemical Bank Report* (52 Broadway, New York, New York 10004, 1983), pp. 30–32.

[2]S. W. Mitchell, *Wear and Tear: Or Hints for the Overworked* (Philadelphia: Lippincott, 8th ed., 1897).

[3]*National Health Interview Survey: U.S. Survey, 1979* (Series 10, no. 136), DHHS Publication number (PHS) 81–1564, April, 1981, pp. 15–16.

[4]Alfred Goodman Gilman, Louis S. Goodman, and Alfred Gilman, *The Pharmacological Basis of Therapeutics,* 6th ed. (New York: Macmillan, 1980).

[5]Yigael Yadin, *Masada* (New York: Random House, 1966), pp. 74–85.

[6]C. A. Ries and M. A. Sahud, "Agranulocytosis Caused by Chinese Herbal Medicines," *Journal of the American Medical Association,* 231(1975):352–355.

[7]Arthritis Foundation, 3400 Peachtree Road, N.E., Atlanta, Georgia 30326.

CHAPTER 10

[1]H. F. Polley, "Evolution of Steroids and Their Value in the Control of Rheumatic Diseases," *Mayo Clinic Proceedings,* (1970)45:1–12.

[2]H. F. Polley and C. H. Slocumb, "Behind the Scenes with Cortisone and ACTH," *Mayo Clinic Proceedings,* 51(1976):471–477.

[3]Ilza Veith, *The Yellow Emperor's Classic of Internal Medicine* (Berkeley and Los Angeles: University of California Press, 1966).

Index